The Bordello Cookbook

A Rollicking Review of America's First Millionaire Madams

The Bordello Cookbook

by Jo Foxworth

with inspired recipes by Jeanne Bauer

MOYER BELL
Wakefield, Rhode Island & London

Published by Moyer Bell

Second Edition

**LIBRARY OF CONGRESS
CATALOGING-IN-PUBLICATION DATA**

Foxworth, Jo
    The bordello cookbook / Jo Foxworth : with recipes by Jeanne Bauer.

p.   cm.
1. Cookery. 2. Prostitution—United States—History—20th century. 3. Prostitutes—United States—History—20th century
I. Bauer, Jeanne. II. Title.
TX714.F69   1999
641.5—dc20   96-15525
ISBN 1-55921-279-9 [Paper]   CIP

Cover illustration by Kathy Crocken
For all art and photograph credits, see the appendix.

Printed in the United States of America
Distributed in North America by Publishers Group West, 1700 Fourth Street, Berkeley, California, 94710, 800-788-3123 (in California 510-528-1444) and in Europe by Gazelle Book Services Ltd., Falcon House, Queen Square, Lancaster LA1 1RN England 524-68765.

This book is dedicated to the memory of the fabulous Everleigh Sisters, Minna and Aida, owners and operators of "the most magnificent bordello in North America," 1900-1911 in Chicago.

THANKS! THANKS! THANKS!

To the friends and business associates who have been helpful to me in putting *The Bordello Cookbook* together:

First of all, Jeanne Voltz, food authority and author of thirteen dynamic cookbooks, who worked with me at the book's inception.

My collaborator, Jeanne Bauer, who developed the extraordinary recipes and related food information herein.

Fifi Oscard, the literary agent who introduced me to my publisher.

Renée Bennett, whose valued counsel and support are always there.

Researchers Claudia Rowe, Shireen Patell, Naeron Verhayen, Tanya Williams, and my niece, Anne Mitchell, the latter a librarian at the University of Texas at Arlington.

Keepers of the flame in my offices: Nobuko Suito, Amy Correia, Jim Skahan, and Evan Gold.

My friend, Betty Thompson, who read the text and held a water gun on me until I changed most of the dashes to commas.

And Buford Hawkins—for Buford knows what!

Finally, I want to thank the twenty-nine publishers who rejected my original proposal for this book. If one of them had been blessed or cursed with the courage to take it on I might never have met Jennifer Moyer, the delightful publisher who did.

—*Jo Foxworth*

CONTENTS

INTRODUCTION

Back when sex was still sin, the house that was not a home had its heyday, and women got their very first break in business.

The homeless house was Big Business, growing out of an obvious need. Respectable wives didn't have orgasms and a respectable husband was alarmed if the woman he had married did. Fun in bed was for men only—and very hard to come by! Any wife who approached sex as more than an onerous duty aroused nothing but suspicion in her husband. When he laughed at the ongoing jokes about the ice man, the Fuller Brush man and the other door-to-door tradesmen, he fervently hoped that he was laughing about the lady next door. His own wife was expected to keep her knickers up and her corset on until he got back home.

At the same time the few jobs available to women were extremely unappealing—especially on payday. Widows and their single sisters found it almost impossible to eke out an honest living and were galled to find themselves dependent on the handouts of grudging relatives. The contributing kin usually expected some tit-for-tat service in return, and the exchange often tilted tit-for-tat into an inequitable balance. A woman who wound up on a relative's doorstep might also wind up functioning as the unpaid *au pair*—baby-sitting, cooking, cleaning, washing and ironing. And in her spare time she could always mend socks, sew on buttons, and wash the dog.

The stage was set for a business that could do something for everybody—men and women, married or not. Enter, Love for Sale!

The turn of the century was the golden age of the American bordello, the only place where it was right and natural for a woman to work and even to be the boss. Women who burned to be something other than housewives could burn themselves to the ground, as far as the male bosses were concerned. In most businesses, nobody female was permitted to darken the door, except maybe to empty the trash, scrub the floor or perform some routine clerical chore that was beneath the dignity of the men. As for the executive suites: "Don't even think about it!"

But at the bordello—ah!—what a difference. A woman at last could run the show, and what a show it was! One could question the taste of the reigning madams but never their imagination. Their flights of fancy gave rise to sex palaces of outrageous splendor, wall-to-wall gauche and gaudery. Everything that glittered adorned the houses: silver and gold, satin and silk, crystal and high gloss bronze. Not to be outdone by their own decor, the madams themselves sparkled with the jewels *du jour*: diamonds, emeralds and rubies, with a few sapphires thrown in to suggest *savoir vivre*. They knew their business right down to the last kink, and Victorian repression actually helped. At this time of reverberating no-noes they understood, first off, that sex alone was not enough. They sensed the need for an aura of make-believe in the sex games that were bought and sold. The unreality of it all created an illusion of escape, an easy out for customers frustrated by propriety and denial at home. A philandering husband could easily put down a guilty conscience by telling himself that none of this was really happening, that he was somebody else in another world.

Although the bordellos were prissily branded "houses of ill repute," many of the more palatial establishments enjoyed a certain cachet, thanks to the business stature and social position of their patrons. A gentleman could keep his family on one side of town and his *filles de joie* on the other, discreetly concealed beneath carved mahogany doors

and opaque windows. Often, the pleasure house of his choice was his alternate club, usually a glitzy mansion endowed with every luxury of the hour, including privacy and police protection. The cover-up was important, it being a time when a man's reputation could be ruined by a sexual scandal that might easily make him a celebrity today.

The bordello was a place where a man could escape a disapproving wife and/or his strait-laced social circles to revel in an evening of total hedonism. Married or single, he valued it as a safe playhouse where he could stash his naughty books and pictures, enjoy his sex toys and have everything his way, without fear of criticism or even a raised eyebrow. He sometimes kept a cache of his own special wines and cigars under lock and key there, and when he was feeling especially expansive ordered exotic game and seafood shipped to the kitchen from faraway places for the enjoyment of the whole establishment. This of course made him the house darling, eligible for all kinds of tricky little treats, including a few freebies.

Some of the houses had twenty-four-hour kitchens whose output often rivaled what was cooking upstairs. Their culinary reputations, it was said, motivated some men to visit particular houses for the food alone. They simply ate heartily and went home. The madams didn't mind if a customer was interested only in the dining room. They happily catered to all kinds of hunger—and the food wasn't cheap either. Even the most elemental houses found that the addition of food and drink was good for business.

Clearly, the madams were not stupid, although some of the girls who worked for them undoubtedly were. Running a bordello was no easier than running one of the great female-generated businesses today—say, Liz Claiborne, Donna Karan or Estee Lauder. A bordello owner had many of the problems current in any successful business plus special headaches that came with the territory.

This is not meant to undercut the brilliant accomplishments of such creators extraordinaire as Claiborne, Karan, and Lauder, or to suggest any personal similarities between them and the dames de bordello, aside from brains, energy, and talent. It is only to underline the fact that the other resources required to start and build a flourishing business were not available to women a hundred years ago, regardless of brains, energy, talent or anything else.

The sex trade was by no means confined to the show-off mansions. In addition to the grand bordellos, there were parlor houses, brothels, sporting houses, cathouses and two-bit cribs. All were lumped together in the mind of the times and commonly called whorehouses— to the intense resentment of madams who ran the "better places."

While there are notes ahead on all types of commercial sex outlets, this book is concerned primarily with the upscale houses and the spectacular women who owned and/or operated them. The records are slim because the business was, after all, illegal and their owners left the dimmest possible trails, both before and after retirement. One of them, who had operated under the fake title of Countess, went to Europe and acquired an authentic title by marrying a real nobleman. Another became the respected and admired mayor of an important city and delighted in publicizing her past. Two others (sisters) moved to New York City where they lived quietly as respectable widows, joining exclusive women's clubs and attending the theatre and opera.

Whatever their lives were later, it is clear that in their salad days, the really successful madams lived in flamboyant (if tasteless) luxury and enjoyed a kind of oblique celebrity. Best of all, they enjoyed the coveted experience of supremacy in business—the kind of heady authority that women may win today. At last.

Obviously, all was not wine and roses in yesterday's whoredom. It wasn't labeled vice for nothing and there were vicious harridans plying the trade who deserved the tragedies that overtook them. This book leaves them to heaven, focusing instead on the characters who were, in some way, truly exceptional. With literally hundreds to choose from I have simply chosen the ones who, to me, were the most interesting. I learned to hate some of these ladies. Maybe you will, too.

But if you don't love the Everleigh Sisters, I'll drink their Champagne Pearadise out of your Reeboks.

— Jo Foxworth

About the food

Recipes and foodstyles in this text are derived from many sources ranging from old family recipes to diary accounts and fond memories. All recipes have been updated to utilize today's food products and kitchen techniques. Where it adds interest, some of the old foods and old ways are included in the text about the recipe. The whorehouse aspect of the food was a fascinating search—a matter of good luck and keen guidance. For their special assistance in the search I am indebted to, among others:

> Johnson & Wales University and its Culinary Archives & Museum; Barbara Kuck, Archivist.
> *Cookery Americana*, Arno Press, New York, 1973. (A series of 27 cookbooks in 15 volumes, chronicling an engaging aspect of American social life over the past 150 years.) And, especially, Louis I. Szathmary, Advisory Editor for the series.

I also want to acknowledge the assistance of the late Maggie Waldron, my dear friend and mentor, and lovingly dedicate my work on this book to her.

—Jeanne Bauer

About the illustrations

Since the bordellos addressed herein were thoroughly damned as both immoral and illegal, the madams welcomed no publicity beyond the testimony of satisfied customers. The ladies of the trade were (understandably) so camera-shy that few authentic photographs survive to commemorate their heyday. We have therefore included only three photographs of famed practitioners: Belle Cora, Lola Montez, and Calamity Jane. Other sketches and pictures scattered throughout the book are not meant to identify any of the people or their places of operation, but only to echo the spirit of the times and the text.

—the editors

The Bordello Cookbook

Food with a Passion

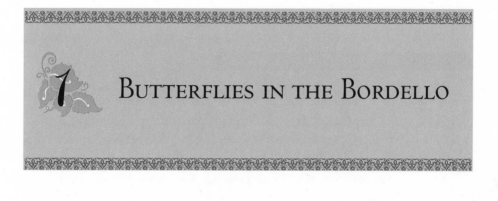

1   BUTTERFLIES IN THE BORDELLO

They could cook, too!

The early madams knew that although the way to a man's heart isn't necessarily through his stomach, it helps to feed him well at the rest stops.

Nobody did it better than the fabulous Everleigh sisters, Minna and Aida, whose Everleigh Club was the showplace of Chicago. Any respectable cookbook about bordellos should certainly begin there because the club was hailed by men (who ought to know) as "the most magnificent bordello in North America." High among its enticements was a twenty-four hour gourmet kitchen whose output was said to rival what was cooking upstairs. Some men swore they dropped by just for the food and if this was really the case, the sisters had no complaints. The charge for dinner was about the same price as a *romp d'amour* upstairs—$50 and up—in 1900 money.

It was Minna's proud boast that everybody who was anybody slept there, including royalty. When Prince Henry of Prussia came to the U.S.A. he announced on landing that the main thing he wanted to do was visit the Everleigh Club. And so he did! During his wild and riotous evening there the Prince was so carried away that he toasted the Everleighs with champagne sipped from a courtesan's silk slipper, thus starting a fad that peaked in the Fitzgerald era and has been known to rise again in the Reebok Age.

The next time some amorous gentleman wants to toast you with champagne, keep your shoes on and serve him this:

Champagne Pearadise

To a glass of chilled, very dry champagne, add a splash of pear brandy (Pear Williams is recommended) and use a long, slim slice of fresh pear as a swizzle stick. Be sure to add just a tiny bit of brandy because the pear aroma and flavor are accentuated by the champagne. (If that doesn't do anything for you, next time try jazzing up the bubbly with a drop of Grand Marnier, Sabra, or another neglected liqueur in your cache of potables.)

Should your gentleman's toast really turn you on, try treating him to a new take on oysters, maybe one of these:

Oyster Purses

Adapted from a popular private club entrée, these tasty appetizers are known to go well with any drinks you're serving, from wine and champagne to beer, stout, and cocktails.

½ pound thinly sliced cooked turkey breast
½ pound thinly sliced cooked ham
1 tablespoon, Dijon-style mustard
6 scallions, long green tops set aside, white part finely
    chopped
24 shucked oysters

Top each slice of turkey with a slice of ham, brush lightly with mustard, and scatter finely chopped scallions over the top. Place an oyster in the center of each, bringing the sides

up to form a purse. Tie each purse with a long green strip
of scallion. Place the oyster purses in a glass dish and
microwave on High for 1 minute, or until heated through.
Serve immediately.

Yield: 24 appetizers

Pickled Oysters

These oyster appetizers are "keepers," or call them make-aheads, which is to say that whenever you find oysters on sale, purchase them, pickle them according to this recipe, and keep them on hand for festive cocktail hours.

3 pints whole oysters, shucked (including liquor)
2 cups white wine vinegar
12 whole cloves
12 whole black peppercorns
2 tablespoons ground mace
2 small red peppers
1 teaspoon salt

Bring the oysters and their liquor to a boil. Remove the oysters to a bowl or jar. Add the vinegar and spices to the oyster liquor, bring to a boil, and pour over the oysters. Cover and let cool. Refrigerate. Serve cold or at room temperature. Crackers or toast points are a good accompaniment.

Yield: 3 pints

According to a nineteenth-century reference called *The Prairie Avenue Cookbook*, "The *bottom* shell is the proper shell in which oysters should be sent to the table; one (often) sees them served in the top shells, which is exceedingly provincial and absolutely wrong." Right or wrong, oysters (especially raw oysters) have enjoyed a long and honorable reputation as an aphrodisiac—a reputation that gains a certain amount of credence from their zinc content. (Zinc, say the avowed experts, stimulates sexual performance.)

This simple sauce is a favorite of true oyster-lovers who feel that the best way to eat them is on the half shell with nothing more than a squeeze of lemon, a bit of grated fresh horseradish, or this simple sauce. According to James Beard, in his *American Cookery* (1972, Little Brown and Company), "If you do not like the natural flavor of oysters, and find that you must cover them with quantities of red cocktail sauce, then perhaps you shouldn't be eating them."

The Everleigh Club was named in honor of the sisters' grandmother who signed her letters to them "Everly Yours." Spelled Everleigh the name was, to them, such a touch of class that they took it as their very own. It suited and it stuck—so well that nobody yet has pinned down the name that the sisters were born with. Their real identity disappeared into the club when it opened for business.

> ## Mignonette Sauce for Raw Oysters
>
> ½ cup red wine vinegar
> 4 tablespoons finely chopped shallots
>
> White pepper and salt to taste
>
> Combine all ingredients in a bowl. To serve, spoon a very little bit over each oyster.
>
> **Note:** *The sauce may be kept refrigerated in a tightly closed container.*
>
> **Yield: 3/4 cup**

The grand opening was February 1, 1900, and the location was 2131 South Dearborn Street in Chicago's ill-famed Levee district. Minna was twenty-one at the time and Aida was twenty-four. Although Minna was the younger, she called the shots; Aida worshipped her and never questioned her decisions.

Chicago was a wide-open city. There were over 500 love-for-sale establishments in the district, all run by veterans of the business, but the young newcomers were unfazed by the competition. It was a "no contest" situation.

The Everleigh Club was a harlot's dream of elegance and sophistication. It was one of the largest mansions in the area and Minna leased it for $500 a month from one Effie Hawkins, a retiring madam who also demanded $55,000 for her tired furnishings. The aged harridan whined that $55,000 (which included goodwill and girls) did not begin to cover her costs but she was willing to make the sacrifice to help a pair of ambitious neophytes. Minna paid her in order to get the house and immediately threw out every scrap of the contents. She then set about creating an interior of unabashed ostentation, with overkill in every detail.

The bedazzling appointments included two curving staircases lined with potted palms and marble statuary, a mammoth ballroom with crystal chandeliers and an Oriental fountain, fourteen reception rooms, thirty-five bedrooms (more appropriately called entertainment parlors), an art gallery hung with tasteful nudes and romantic pastoral paintings, a music room for weekly musicales, and a library filled with leather-bound classics. There were Gold, Silver, and Copper parlors reserved for the mining magnates whose wealth approached that of the oil sheiks. The Gold Parlor was adorned with eighteen-carat gold spittoons, gold-rimmed fishbowls, and gold-plated sconces. There were also color-themed rooms; Japanese, Chinese, and Egyptian rooms; and the mandatory Moorish room.

Minna quickly fired the crude, used-up whores who had worked for Effie, replacing them with the freshest, prettiest girls she could find. Since the sisters were self-declared Southern belles, Minna also fired the slovenly white servants, hiring instead a staff of well-trained, white-gloved blacks to enhance the genteel atmosphere of the South that was to be the club's hallmark. A Chicago historian described the Everleigh Club soiree as a dazzling affair—gold-rimmed china, crystal glassware, silver and gold cutlery, gold trays and champagne buckets, tablecloths of Irish linen and Spanish lace. All this in a dining room paneled in walnut and containing a mahogany refectory table large enough to seat fifty. The Pullman Buffet, a reproduction in mahogany of a section of a railroad dining car, was used for smaller affairs. It was equally lavish—just smaller.

The club employed from fifteen to twenty-five cooks. Parties, for which the house was famous, were prepared by a *Cordon Bleu* chef. A meal with wine began at $50 and cost rose according to the rarity of dishes ordered. The price did not include a girl. The most expensive party ever at the club was a supper for six, honoring a railroad president. Every dish was an out-of-season delicacy and the price was over $2,000 per person—in 1912 money!

Every night was special at the Everleigh Club, but Butterfly Night was the *pièce de résistance*. Nobody knew when **Butterfly Night** would be but anybody lucky enough to be there when it happened never forgot it. Both sisters had been influenced in their teens by the pre-Raphaelite poets and Minna, especially, had a romantic turn of mind. When the mood was upon her, she released swarms of butterflies into the club's public areas. Suddenly, colorful swirls of them materialized as if by magic, flitting though a wonderland of Victorian gaudery. The delicate creatures hovered over Aida's $15,000 gold-plated piano, the gold

cloth upholstery and draperies, the marble statues of "Grecian Goddesses," then headed upstairs—as a bordello butterfly should.

Minna's Butterfly Nights were inspiration for a lot of romantic little dinners at the club, which can be replicated by the hostess whose home is not a house.

To make a routine occasion memorable, you might do the table in a butterfly motif and mesmerize your guests with tales of the Everleigh Sisters. Butterfly Night was always festive, inventive, and most of all fun. Surprise was the quality that prevailed and menus teased both the mind and the palate. Your own butterfly dinner could be an unforgettable occasion with a menu like this:

Bordello Cocktails
Hors d'oeuvres Everleigh
Lobster Bisque Aida
Minna's Roast Capon with Wild Rice and Pecan Stuffing
Hearts of Palm Salad
Ginger Bombe

A WORD ABOUT COCKTAILS

Although the science of distillation was known to the ancient Egyptians, the cocktail is a purely American institution, originated for the purpose of appetite-whetting. The clever Everleighs knew more about appetite-whetting than most people and exploited their knowledge in every area of the club.

Minna's Clover Cocktail

¾ ounce lemon juice

1½ ounces dry gin

1 teaspoon grenadine syrup

Shake all the ingredients together thoroughly with cracked ice and strain into a cocktail glass.

Yield: 1 cocktail

South Dearborn Street Tropical Punch

(Icebreaker for a crowd)

2 quarts dark rum

1 quart brandy

1 cup peach liqueur

1 quart lemon juice

2 cups sugar

2 quarts cold water

One 5-pound bag ice cubes

Place all the ingredients in a large punch bowl, stir, and allow to stand for at least 2 hours. Stir before serving. Add more ice for a less potent punch.

Yield: about 1½ gallons

APPETIZER BOUQUETS

"A treat for the eyes as well as the palate" was the way the Everleigh Club's famous "Appetizer Bouquet" was referred to. First-timers were titillated by the descriptives used, but no guest ever dared ask what actually was in the "bouquets." Now you know what all the fuss was about, and why these rose butter delights were served only with champagne. They're too delicate to be served with any other beverage.

Rose Butter Canapes

1 stick sweet butter, cut into 12 pieces
Rose petals from 6 very fragrant roses
1 small loaf white cocktail bread, thinly sliced
Roses, for garnish

Place the butter in a jar with a tight lid, and top with the rose petals. Cover and keep tightly closed for several hours, or until the petals are withered. Remove the petals. Cream the butter and spread on thin slices of bread, placing 2 buttered slices together. Cut into ribbons, squares, rounds, or triangles. Garnish with roses and/or more rose petals.

Yield: ½ cup filling

And for a more "he-man" cocktail spread, try:

ROQUEFORT SPREAD PRINCE HENRY

1/2 cup Roquefort cheese
1/4 cup sweet butter
1/4 cup cream cheese
2 tablespoons brandy
1/2 teaspoon dry mustard

Cream the Roquefort, butter, and cream cheese together until well combined. Add the brandy and mustard. Spoon into a jar with a tight-fitting cover. Cover and refrigerate for several hours. (May be kept, refrigerated, for a week.) Use as a spread on toast fingers or to fill tiny puff pastries.

Yield: 1 cup filling

Minna's Stuffed Roast Capon

One 6- to 8-pound capon
1 cup cooked wild rice
1 cup chopped pecans
½ cup finely chopped onion
½ cup finely chopped apple
1 egg, well beaten
½ cup chopped fresh parsley
Salt and pepper to taste

Preheat oven to 425°F.

Rinse the capon inside and out and pat dry. In a large bowl, mix the remaining ingredients together, tossing lightly to combine. Spoon the stuffing loosely into the capon and truss. Place in a roasting pan and roast for 15 minutes; reduce heat to 350°F. and continue roasting for another 1 ½ to 2 hours. Remove the trussing strings and slice into servings.

Yield: 6 to 8 servings

Hearts of Palm Salad

2 (14-ounce) cans hearts of palm, drained
¼ cup extra virgin olive oil
2 tablespoons lemon juice
Freshly ground black pepper
1 tablespoon minced fresh tarragon
¼ cup thinly sliced pimiento

Halve the hearts of palm lengthwise and arrange in a large flat-bottomed dish. Drizzle evenly with the olive oil and lemon juice. Sprinkle black pepper and tarragon over all; cover and let marinate in the refrigerator for several hours, turning several times. Serve on a bed of crisp greens, and garnish with pimiento slices.

Yield: 6 servings

The history of Minna and Aida Everleigh is difficult to document because the elusive pair literally invented themselves. Their lives were built on fantasy, fiction, and colorful lies—a web of cheerful deceit that obscures their early years and those that followed their retirement. It was their eleven-year reign as queens of the bordello business that the world remarks to this day—the time of their lives in Chicago!

According to the few sketchy records that survive, when Minna was eighteen and Aida was twenty-one they married two brothers named Lester whose brutish behavior might have caused them to relish the exploitation of men that became their life's work. The Lesters were so abusive that after less than a year of unholy wedlock the brides ran away and went on the stage. The road show they joined produced garment-rending melodramas—such tiresome turkeys that they were looking around for career alternatives when a windfall landed in the wings. Their father died and left them $35,000, which in those days was a tidy fortune. The road show was playing Omaha when they got their hands on the money and they began looking for investment opportunities there. Learning that the big money was being made in the parlor houses, they bought a rundown brothel near Omaha's Trans-Mississippi Exposition, which was attracting huge crowds. Minna, the brains of the business, brightened the place up with fresh paint and wallpaper, and began offering the customers excellent food and imported wine.

Omaha has always been a meat and potatoes town and what we know as Yankee pot roast was a staple of the times. It was glorified with names like "Beef à la Mode," "Étouffée of Beef," "Daube Provençale," and "Bordelaise of Beef," which gave it extra appeal. The benefits of pot roast remain high today—the best cuts being inexpensive ones like rump, round, and chuck—and the same trick to making it appear fancier still applies. Have the butcher roll and tie the meat so you get a better-looking roast and more compact slices of meat. Another plus—as a general rule, pot roasts are better if cooked one day, left to cool, and reheated the next day. A modern advantage of this process is that it's a healthy way to remove excess fat from the sauce.

Brandied Beef

1 teaspoon dried thyme
1 teaspoon dried rosemary
1 teaspoon salt
1½ teaspoons pepper
5- to 6-pound rump, chuck, or round roast, rolled and tied
2 slices bacon, cubed
½ cup brandy
2 cloves garlic, split
1 bay leaf
2 cups dry red wine
2 cups beef broth
8 to 10 carrots, peeled and halved
8 to 10 small potatoes, peeled and halved

THE BORDELLO COOKBOOK

1 package (9-ounce) frozen artichoke hearts
½ pound mushrooms, cleaned and halved
¼ cup chopped parsley

Combine the seasonings in a small bowl. Rub the roast with the seasoning and set aside. In a 5- to 6-quart Dutch oven, sauté the bacon and remove. Add the roast to the pan, browning it on all sides. Remove pot from flame. Pour the brandy over the roast and ignite. When the flame subsides, add the garlic bay leaf, red wine, and beef broth. Bring mixture to a boil, reduce the heat to a simmer, and cook, covered, for 1½ hours. Add the carrots and potatoes; cover and simmer for another 45 minutes. Let cool. Remove the meat and vegetables from the gravy. Refrigerate for several hours or overnight. (To remove excess fat from the gravy prior to serving, use a spoon to scrape congealed fat from the top of the gravy.) Gently reheat the pot roast in the gravy, adding the carrots and potatoes plus the artichokes and mushrooms to the mixture after the roast has heated through. Cover and cook over low heat only until mushrooms and artichokes have been heated through, about 10 to 15 minutes. Do not overcook. Place the meat on a platter and surround it with the vegetables. Sprinkle chopped parsley over all.

Yield: 8 to 10 servings

Potato Pancakes

1 pound russet potatoes, scrubbed
1 large onion
3 eggs
2 tablespoons flour
1 teaspoon salt
½ teaspoon white pepper
1 tablespoon vegetable oil

In a food processor, grate the potatoes and onion; transfer to a large bowl and add the eggs, one at a time. Stir in flour, salt, and pepper. In a nonstick skillet, heat the oil until very hot. Add the potato mixture, ½ cup at a time, spreading it to make a very thin pancake. Cook until golden brown, about 2 minutes; turn and cook on second side until golden. Repeat with remaining potato mixture. Serve hot.

Yield: 8 servings

Note: *Great served with applesauce or applesauce with a tablespoon of horseradish added!*

The addition of food and wine to the sisters' parlor-house menu in Omaha was a prophetic touch. The johns loved it!—and in less than two years the young madams had doubled their money.

That did it! Obviously, the sex trade was for them. It was their big chance for the stardom they had dreamed about, and they now had the funds to set the stage. They set it in Chicago, hub city of the nation—Boomtown, U.S.A.—center of operations for the cattle barons, the silver and copper kings, assorted sports figures, and dandies of every stripe. Even Al Capone! Minna and Aida took the city's measure and set out to measure up. The world had never seen such a place as the Everleigh Club and the news of it sped around the globe. It traveled via the most enticing advertising of all—word of mouth. What man could fail to broadcast his adventures on canopied beds that sprayed exotic perfume on him and a cavorting companion? Or mattressed Persian rugs that transported an impetuous frolic on the floor into an hour of Islamic splendor?

Such adventures inspired recipes that even made their way to Perry Street and the very proper homes of Chicago's elite—the Marshall Fields, the Armours, and the Kelloggs.

The Bordello Cookbook

HAUNCH OF VENISON

Venison and other game were wildly popular and considered somewhat of a delicacy. The "haunch" referred to in the old cookbooks was an ungainly cut. But today's venison is neater, often farm-raised, and much less gamy in taste. (One old-time recipe book started the venison section this way: "Wash your haunch clean, and lay it in a dry cloth; put it in a tin pan, then pour over it a half pint of red wine; rub with cayenne, salt, mace and nutmeg. Let sit overnight.") Venison was never served without a sauce. The reason is quite obvious. The following venison recipe makes its own delicious sauce.

Mackinac Island Venison Filets

1½ cups dry red wine
¼ cup dried cranberries
4 tablespoons extra virgin olive oil, divided
1 teaspoon coarsely ground black pepper
four 5-ounce venison filets

2 tablespoons butter

Combine the wine, 2 tablespoons of the olive oil, cranberries, and pepper in a shallow glass pan; add venison. Cover, refrigerate, and marinate for 24 hours, turning several times. Melt the butter and remaining 2 tablespoons olive oil in a large fry pan over medium heat. Remove venison from the marinade and add to the fry pan. Sauté until golden brown, about 2 minutes per side. Remove venison to a heated serving platter. Add marinade to the fry pan and cook over high heat until the marinade is reduced to about $1/3$ cup. Top warm venison filets with sauce.

Yield: 4 servings

The chafing dish hit its stride in popularity in Chicago and elsewhere during this period. Interest in food had moved from the kitchen and feeding the family to interest in lavish dining and entertaining guests. For the madam, the chafing dish not only added a look of elegance, it kept the entrées warm for the requisite extended period.

The Crab Newburg (a.k.a. Newbourgh) of the times called for a rich fresh crabmeat, sherried white sauce made with butter, cream, and egg yolks. This modern version is "lighter" and also less costly because we've substituted surimi for fresh crab—surimi being the tasty mixture of pike and other fish which are ground and shaped into crabmeat look-alikes. Sauced as it is you really can't tell the difference. This remains a party dish. Elegant and rich-tasting, it smacks of the "high living" prevalent during the Everleigh sisters' reign.

"Crab" Newburg (a microwave version)

1 teaspoon butter
1½ cups skim milk
one 4-ounce package light cream cheese, softened
½ teaspoon white pepper

1 tablespoon sherry
1 pound surimi, flaked
Paprika, for garnish

Place all the ingredients, except the surimi and paprika, in a glass bowl, cover, and microwave on Medium for about 2 minutes. Stir to a smooth consistency. Fold in the surimi. Cover and cook on Medium for 30 seconds, or until heated through. Serve over toast points or rice. Garnish with a sprinkling of paprika.

Yield: 4 servings

Charlotte Russe

Charlotte Russe became the American hostess's most glamorous dessert in the late nineteenth century. The dessert is rumored to have been created by a French confectioner, Careme, and supposedly resembled a French hat style popular at the time. Whatever the origins of the name, the dessert still is a crowd-pleaser, albeit a high-calorie one.

18 ladyfingers
½ cup light rum (*framboise* or kirsch may be substituted)
1 quart prepared vanilla pudding
¼ teaspoon almond extract
1 cup heavy cream
¼ cup confectioners' sugar
1 teaspoon vanilla extract
1 cup dark cherry jam or preserves

Brush the ladyfingers with rum; line the sides of a 2-quart glass bowl with ladyfingers, flat side against the glass. To the vanilla pudding, add the almond extract. Spoon the pudding into the prepared bowl. Cover and refrigerate for 2 to 3 hours.

Whip the cream with the sugar and vanilla until soft peaks

form. Using a pastry bag and star tube, pipe a wide ring of whipped cream around the edge of the dessert. Mound the cherry jam in the center. Cover and refrigerate for at least an hour before cutting.

Yield: 8 to 10 servings

Both sisters had gourmet tastes and a conviction that food and sex are inseparable, the essence of life itself. Since Minna was a stickler for both mystery and imagination, she enjoyed joining the chef in creating dishes that could be inspired choices for the next entertaining little soiree you plan for very special friends. Game of all sorts could be found on the Everleigh buffet table and since game birds are now available year round, even at the supermarket, a good choice would be pheasant, which was a favorite of Minna's. The following recipe was one she initially created with wild pheasant supplied by a hunter who was a generous Everleigh guest (but chicken breast works just as well).

Wild rice was the usual accompaniment for this dish. Try spiking it with a touch of gin and fresh dill, just for fun (and flavor).

Most food historians will agree that this recipe would have been popular just because of the name. But it was wildly fashionable in America, although some think it was adapted from an old English dish. Served Everleigh-style, these cutlets became popular midnight snacks.

Pheasant Supreme Everleigh

6 pheasant (or chicken) breast cutlets
1 teaspoon salt
½ teaspoon white pepper
1 tablespoon butter
1 tablespoon olive oil
½ cup chopped shallots
½ cup dry white wine
1 cup light sour cream
1 tablespoon prepared horseradish
Parsley, for garnish

The Bordello Cookbook

Season the cutlets evenly with the salt and pepper. Melt the butter and olive oil in a large skillet. Sauté the cutlets over medium heat for 5 minutes per side, or until lightly browned. Remove the cutlets to a shallow oven-proof dish, placing them in a single layer. Cover with pan drippings and chopped shallots and white wine. Roast at 350°F. for 15 to 20 minutes, or until just tender. Remove the cutlets to a warm platter. Add the sour cream and horseradish to the pan juices, stirring constantly. Heat thoroughly over low heat, taking care that the sour cream does not separate. Spoon the sauce over the cutlets and garnish with the parsley.

Yield: 6 servings

Asparagus in Ambush

6 to 8 rectangular French rolls (about 6 inches long)
3 pounds fresh asparagus, cleaned and trimmed
1 large red pepper, cleaned, cored, cut into 6 or 8 1-inch strips
1 teaspoon dried dill
1 teaspoon white wine vinegar
Pinch salt
Pinch sugar
½ teaspoon Dijon-style mustard
½ cup light sour cream

Split the French rolls and remove the soft crumb from the insides. Toast the rolls and tops lightly and keep warm. Blanch the asparagus and red pepper (a microwave oven makes quick work of it) and keep warm. Combine the remaining ingredients, mixing well to combine. When ready to serve, place the asparagus and red pepper strips in hollowed rolls, alternating red and green colors. Drizzle dill sauce over vegetables. Cover the rolls with the tops. Drizzle remaining sauce over tops of the rolls. Serve immediately.

Yield: 6 to 8 servings

From the Everleighs' celebrated kitchen, a late supper was served to guests and the girls they had chosen for the evening. Their selections were made from an elaborate menu that from time to time listed: fresh caviar, oysters, lobster, pheasant, beef rib roast, capon, squab, guinea fowl, duck, rack of lamb, Welsh rarebit, and a gamut of fresh vegetables, salads, and desserts. On special occasions, there was even baked stuffed swan, offered mainly because it sounded exotic. "Impressive," sniffed Minna, "but a bit stringy." These little suppers cost $50 and up per person and only a cad would refuse to pay the tab for his paramour.

Since February is the dreariest month of the year in most places, you might think about doing something to cheer things up. Why not get a few friends together to celebrate the anniversary of the Everleigh's opening (February 1, 1900) with a dinner inspired by the club's extraordinary chef.

"Fools" were a dime a dozen in America at the turn of the century. The term is used to describe just-cooked, puréed fruit served with cream. This recipe uses what was called spring fruit or pie plant. It's rhubarb, of course, and it grew wild and cultivated all over the Midwest. The first "fool" of the year was, no doubt, rhubarb, and fools moved through the seasons to include berries and other tree fruits of the area. We like this one because of the color—pale pinkish red—and the flavor contrast of the sweet-tart fruit and the cool, smooth cream. Serve in a stemmed sherbet dish and top with a candied violet. Applause.

Rhubarb Fool (a microwave version)

4 cups chopped rhubarb
$^2/_3$ cup honey
¼ cup water
1 cup whipping cream
Candied violets, for garnish

Microwave instructions: In a 4-quart microwave-safe casserole, combine rhubarb, honey, and water. Cook, covered, on High for 7 to 8 minutes. Let stand, covered, for another 10 minutes. Let cool to room temperature. Process in a food processor until smooth. Refrigerate until chilled. Whip cream until stiff peaks form. Fold in rhubarb purée until thoroughly combined. Spoon into sherbet glasses. Refrigerate until serving. Garnish with candied violets.

Yield: 4 to 6 servings

Note: The "parfait" was a trendy dessert of the times, and you can turn the "fool" into a parfait by alternating rhubarb purée and whipped cream in a tall parfait glass.

A reporter for the *Chicago Tribune* who enjoyed the club's delights both upstairs and down declared that "the Everleighs are to entertainment what Christ was to Christianity." The fulsomeness of his praise was understandable if not in the best of taste. One of Minna's laws decreed that no member of the working press was ever to pay a dime for anything—food, booze, or girls. Consequently, news items about the club received cautious if not tender treatment. Also, the Everleigh's phone number, Calumet 412, was always handy to the *Chicago Tribune*'s night editor in case he needed reporters to help with late-breaking stories. (Once, when word was flashed to the *Tribune* night desk that the Everleigh Club was on fire, the editor went looking for reporters to cover the blaze, only to find that his three top men were already there, happily engaged upstairs.)

The sisters never turned a trick themselves. Their private quarters were strictly off-limits to guests, and the only people ever admitted were Chicago officials with whom they maintained warm friendships, kindled by huge payoffs.

Both sisters circulated through the drawing rooms each evening, but Minna was always the center of attention. She was a striking redhead with blue eyes and thin, refined features. She wore silk evening gowns, a large diamond necklace, a profusion of bracelets, rings, and an ornamental girdle called a stomacher, ablaze with rubies and emeralds. Edgar Lee Masters, author of the *Spoon River Anthology*, and a club regular, wrote unflatteringly that "her walk was a sort of caterpillar bend and hump, pause and catch up."

Responsibility for Minna's caterpillar walk has been attributed to that ornamental girdle, which was inspiration for the name of this amusing party dessert:

Girdled Strawberries

Choose the biggest, reddest strawberries you can find, wash them, and serve in little bowls with pots of fondue. Leave the stems on and let your guests have the fun of dipping their own—"girdling" them in white or traditional chocolate fondue—or both! You may also serve orange segments, slices of peaches or pears, or whatever; and in winter you can dip dried apricots, pears, peaches, and so on.

White Fondue

1 pound white chocolate, chopped
1 cup half-and-half
1 tablespoon Grand Marnier

The Bordello Cookbook

Chocolate Fondue

1 pound bittersweet chocolate, chopped
1 cup half-and-half
1 tablespoon cognac

To make each fondue: Melt the chocolate with ½ cup of the half-and-half in a heat-proof dish over very low heat (or on low power in the microwave) until chocolate is melted. Stir in liquor and remaining half-and-half as needed to bring the mixture to a good dipping consistency. Pour into warmed fondue pots or chafing dishes. Guests select the fruit and dip as little or as much as they'd like to "girdle" the fruit.

Note: *In summer, place the fruit in the freezer for about 15 minutes before dipping—it makes the fondue adhere better!*

Caterpillar walk notwithstanding, Minna was a delightful hostess whose manner was that of the committee chairwoman at an especially festive cotillion. Aida, though quieter and more soft-spoken, was also a charming hostess—gracious, solicitous, and warm—especially effective with young customers and men visiting a bordello for the first time. She had a happy way of making newcomers feel at home in a strange new environment and this was helped along with Everleigh foods like the ones that follow:

Oyster Stew

Yes, the pleasure palaces had their own form of "comfort food"—homey and familiar, it was still served with a certain amount of flair.

2 tablespoons butter
2 carrots, finely chopped
1 medium potato, finely chopped

2 small onions, finely chopped
2 stalks celery, finely chopped
1 cup milk
1 dozen shucked oysters, including the liquor
Dash of hot pepper
1 cup half-and-half

In a medium saucepan, melt butter, add vegetables, and sauté until tender, stirring often. Add milk and bring to a boil. Add oysters and their liquor and bring to a boil to plump oysters. Season with salt and hot pepper sauce. Add half-and-half and bring to a point just below boiling, stirring constantly. Serve immediately.

Yield: 2 servings

Rice Pudding à la Rhum

½ cup golden raisins
½ cup dark rum
5 eggs
2 cups milk
1 teaspoon vanilla extract
½ teaspoon salt
2½ cups cooked rice
½ cup sugar
Ground nutmeg, for garnish

In a small bowl, soak raisins in rum for at least 1 hour. In a medium bowl, beat together eggs, milk, vanilla, and salt. Stir in rice, sugar, and raisin–rum mixture. Pour into a buttered 2-quart baking dish. Bake at 350°F. for 30 to 40 minutes, or until pudding is firm to the touch and lightly browned on top. Before serving, sprinkle top lightly with nutmeg. Serve warm or at room temperature.

Yield: 6 servings

From 1900 until 1911 the club flourished. This period, of course, was Chicago's notorious Gangster Era and, while there are no newspaper accounts linking the mob to the Everleigh, there is little doubt that some of Capone's boys were regulars at the elegant club. There is also no doubt whatever that those of them who did visit the Everleigh were on their best Sunday school behavior. The sisters allowed no ungentlemanly conduct and insisted that the girls who lived there maintain absolutely ladylike behavior beyond the bedrooms.

In her orientation lecture to new recruits Minna urged them to be polite and patient and remember that one $50 client is more desirable than five $10 ones. "Less wear and tear," she said. "You will thank me for this advice in later years. Your youth and beauty are all you have. Preserve it. Stay respectable by all means. We will supply the clients. You amuse them in a way that they have never been amused before. Give—but interestingly and with mystery. I want you girls to be proud you're in the Everleigh Club." Proud they were. Residence there was considered the ultimate achievement in the profession. One jealous madam in the Levee district complained that "every whore in America wants to work at the Everleigh."

The girls ate lavishly, it being the sisters' belief that good eating sparked good performance. A sumptuous breakfast was served to them at two o'clock in the afternoon in the club's main dining room. The meal always began with cold clam juice and an aspirin, the house "cure" for the effects of an evening of indulgence. This was followed typically by such delights as these:

Shad Roe (in season)

Planked Whitefish

Sautéed Kidneys with Bacon Curls

Clam Cakes

Breast of Chicken

Choice of Eggs and Toast

Tea or Turkish Coffee

Sunday brunch, always a popular form of entertainment, has lately grown ho-hum if not boring. Make it exciting again by inviting friends over for a midday bordello buffet. You might base your menu on selections from the above. Or even haul out the chafing dish and try some interesting flamers, followed by hearty fare like steak and eggs and other stockyard favorites with exotic new touches. Here's a keep-'em-happy meal to brighten up Sunday, with recipes that have been healthfully lightened up.

Although the term "brunch," did not enter everybody's vocabulary until the 1930s, this weekend midday meal was "guaranteed to be jam-packed at the house." Where else could a fellow get such great hangover remedies, followed by grand food? Followed by a nice nap and whatever.

We've selected some favorites of the day—some nearly forgotten. First, a beverage:

Gin Buck

Right out of the Prohibition era! The secret is the lemon shell added to the drink.

1½ ounces gin
½ lemon
Ginger ale
Lemon shell

Serve "short" or "long," depending on the season. Juice the lemon, reserving the shell. Start with ice cubes in a glass; add gin, lemon juice, and lemon shell. Top off with ginger ale. Makes 1 hangover cure. Serve no more than 2 per customer.

Yield: 1 drink

Mushroom Omelet

1½ cups cholesterol-free eggs
¼ cup skim milk

4 egg whites, stiffly beaten
Dash of hot sauce
Pinch white pepper
2 pounds mushrooms, sliced
½ cup sliced scallions
Salt and pepper to taste

Fold cholesterol-free eggs, milk, hot sauce, and pepper into stiffly beaten egg whites. Pour in heated nonstick skillet, lifting bottom often to be sure it doesn't burn. (You may want to spray the skillet with a no-cholesterol spray first.) Serve mushroom sauce on top or fold inside omelet.

To make mushroom sauce/filling: Cook mushrooms, scallions, and seasonings over low heat, covered, in a nonstick skillet until softened and heated through. Moisture from the mushrooms will form enough liquid so you won't have to add any fat. Serve immediately in or over the omelet.

Yield: 4 servings

Peking Beef Strips

1 cup sliced sweet onions
1 cup bean sprouts, rinsed and drained
1 clove garlic, minced
½ cup rice vinegar
¼ cup sugar
1 pound lean beef, cut into 2 x ½-inch strips
½ cup low-salt soy sauce
½ cup julienned orange peel
1 teaspoon grated fresh ginger
½ teaspoon crushed Szechuan peppers (or black peppercorns)

In a large bowl, marinate onions, bean sprouts, garlic, vinegar and sugar for at least 30 minutes, stirring to coat.

Brown beef strips in non-stick skillet with a teaspoon of the marinade. Add remaining ingredients and toss to heat through and blend ingredients. Serve beef over a bed of drained onion/bean sprout mixture. Serve immediately.

Yield: 4 servings

The Everleigh sisters' profits averaged $10,000 a month until the club encountered an intractable crackdown on vice. A new reform-minded mayor, Carter Harrison, was at first reluctant to close down one of the city's major tourist attractions—which the Everleigh Club had become. But then one day an aide showed him a brochure that the Everleigh was distributing, describing its glories in deep-breathing detail. The blatancy of this advertising was too much for Harrison who summoned his police chief and aldermen, commanding them to shut down the Everleigh at once. On October 24, 1911, Minna and Aida were notified that it was all over. Emmett Murphy, author of *Great Bordellos of the World*, wrote that the police officer who formally closed the club was fittingly named Captain John McWeeny.

Next October, you can turn your big entertainment of the season into the party of the decade by declaring it a memorial to the Everleigh's closing. Send invitations three weeks ahead announcing that it is to be a costume party, with prizes for winning costumes.

Menu Ideas for an
EVERLEIGH MEMORIAL DINNER
(Choose from the Everleigh list)

Slings, Swizzles, and Rickies	Coriandered Artichokes*
Tomato Bisque	Spinach Deluxe
Egg Variations	Macedoine Salad
Duck Hash*	Salad Variations
Soused Swordfish*	Fruit Pies
Bavarian Pork Roast*	Angel and Devil's Food Cakes
Potato Pancakes	Assorted Candies and Ice Creams
Potato and Rice Variations	Brandy Alexander Pie*

*Recipes follow

SLINGS, SWIZZLES, AND RICKIES

Sexy drinks of the Everleigh era make for great conversation, if only for their great names: *Slings* are really sweet Old Fashioneds—equal amounts of powdered sugar and lemon juice plus liquor (brandy, gin, vodka, or whiskey). Just add a twist of lemon and serve on the rocks. *Swizzles* originated in the West Indies, where a twig with several forked branches on the end was used as a stirrer, or swizzle stick. A basic mixture of lime, bitters, sugar, and booze (brandy, gin, rum, and whiskey) is poured over a large glass of shaved or crushed ice. *Rickies*, a cross between a Collins and a Sour, always contain lime, cracked ice, and a carbonated beverage to make a long, tall drink. Gin, rum, scotch, vodka, whiskey—you name it, it was used to make a Rickey of some sort. One of the more famous drinks of the day was the *Fog Horn*. It was a dry gin Rickey. We strongly suspect it was a coastal drink.

Duck Hash

As one story goes, this fabulous dish was originally made from leftover duck, but it became such a favorite of one of Chicago's finest that he actually took up duck hunting in order to provide the main ingredient for his favorite of all dishes at the Everleigh Club. It's a real pleaser, a robust and delectable entrée.

3 cups (1-inch cubed pieces) cooked duck meat
½ cup dry red wine
½ cup currant jelly
3 tablespoons butter, divided
2 cups coarsely shredded cabbage
2 cups coarsely shredded potato
1 cup chopped onion
2 teaspoons salt
1 teaspoon coarsely ground black pepper
1 cup dry bread crumbs
1 teaspoon dried coriander

In a large bowl, combine duck meat, red wine, and currant jelly, tossing to coat well. Set aside. In a large skillet, heat 1 tablespoon of the butter. Add cabbage and cook over medium heat for 5 to 8 minutes, or until transparent. Add cabbage to duck meat mixture, tossing to combine. In the same skillet, melt the remaining 2 tablespoons butter, add potato and onions; and cook over medium heat for 10 to 12 minutes, until softened and lightly browned. Add to duck mixture, tossing to combine. Season mixture with salt and pepper and spoon the duck mixture into a cast-iron skillet, packing it firmly. In a small bowl, combine bread crumbs and coriander; sprinkle over the top of the duck hash. Bake at 350°F. about 20 minutes. Brown top under broiler for 2 to 3 minutes. Serve immediately.

Yield: 6 to 8 servings

Soused Swordfish

1 quart dark beer
1 carrot, sliced
1 onion, sliced
1 stalk celery, sliced
¼ cup chopped fresh parsley
8 peppercorns
5 whole cloves
1 bay leaf
Eight 6-ounce swordfish steaks

In a large skillet, bring all ingredients, except fish, to a boil. Reduce heat, cover, and simmer 15 to 20 minutes. Place fish in skillet to fit in one layer. (Liquid should cover fish completely.) Cover and simmer for about 15 minutes, or until fish flakes easily when tested with a fork. Remove fish from poaching liquid, drain, and serve immediately.

Yield: 8 servings

Bavarian Pork Roast

One 4- to 5-pound boneless pork loin, tied, a pocket cut
    along length of the roast
1 teaspoon salt
1 teaspoon cracked black pepper
1 cup Riesling wine
1 cup pitted prunes
1 tablespoon butter
1 cup chopped onion
1 clove garlic, chopped
6 slices caraway rye bread, cubed (or substitute plain rye plus
    1 teaspoon caraway seeds)

Season pork loin with salt and pepper. Bring wine to a boil,
pour over prunes, and steep about 30 minutes, or until
softened. Melt butter in a medium skillet, add onion and
garlic, and sauté until soft and transparent. Add bread cubes,
tossing to combine.

Insert prunes in pork pocket, distributing evenly. Add any
wine remaining to the bread mixture. Tuck bread mixture
into pocket over prunes. Tie the loin in several places to
keep its shape. Roast at 350°F. for 1 to 1½ hours, or until
meat thermometer reads 140°F. Do not overcook. Remove
roast from oven and let rest at room temperature for about
10 minutes before carving. Serve immediately.

Yield: 6 to 8 servings

Coriandered Artichokes

Exotic spices (coriander was one such sexy flavor) were
considered somewhat wicked to the midwestern palate in
Chicago. Yes, the Everleigh sisters used these spices sparingly
but well. Here's an example:

8 large artichokes, cleaned and trimmed
Boiling salted water
8 coriander seeds
2 lemons, sliced

Drop the artichokes into boiling salted water to cover. Add coriander seeds and lemon slices. Simmer, covered, until artichokes are tender, about 40 minutes. Drain well, inverted. Serve hot at room temperature, or chilled.

Yield: 8 servings

Quick tip: To cook in the microwave, wrap artichokes individually in plastic wrap along with whatever water clings after rinsing, 1 coriander seed and a slice of lemon. Cook on HIGH for 6 to 10 minutes, depending on how many artichokes are cooked at one time. Let stand, wrapped, for about 5 minutes before serving.

Side dishes, out of necessity, had to look good on the buffet table and taste good for quite a long time—until the last guest (who might have been busy upstairs, or wherever) had filled his plate. Several culinary "tricks" were devised to keep the food looking freshly prepared even hours after the buffet had begun. For vegetables, for instance, spinach deluxe meant spinach that had been topped by finely chopped egg. The trick: When the dish looked tired, more spinach was added and the remaining chopped egg mixed right in—it didn't even show. What was critical was to cover the entire dish once again with a pristine chopped egg. Yes, the dish became pretty "eggy" after a while. But there are those who preferred the spinach with lots of chopped hard-cooked egg, and those were the ones found coming back at the last minutes of the buffet for their spinach fix.

Another side-dish trick had to do more with the name than anything. Lots of *macedoine* was served during the Everleigh's reign. Macedoine looks good on the menu, but it merely means a mixture of vegetables or fruit, cut into small dice. The macedoine salad or vegetable often started out the evening with an original mixture, and as the buffet went on into the hours, it was "added to" in interesting and often inventive ways. Some terrific combinations were created out of necessity, and the name of the dish always was correct and enticing—a macedoine.

Brandy Alexander Pie

The original version of this dessert was pretty labor intensive. Today's version goes together in much less time, so it's much more fun to serve.

1 package (8½ ounce) chocolate wafers
4 tablespoons butter, melted
2 tablespoons brandy, plus ¼ cup brandy
2 cups chocolate pudding (made from a mix or already
      prepared)
¼ cup chocolate-flavored liqueur
1 cup whipping cream, whipped
1 ounce semisweet chocolate (optional)

Place chocolate wafers in food processor and process until finely crumbed. Combine crumbs with butter and two tablespoons brandy, mixing well. Press into bottom and up sides of a 9-inch pie pan. Set aside.

In a large bowl, combine chocolate pudding, liqueur, and brandy, stirring to combine; fold in whipped cream gently. Spoon into crumb crust, smoothing top. Cover and refrigerate for at least 1 hour before serving. To garnish, make chocolate curls by using a vegetable peeler on the flat, smooth side of the chocolate square; scatter curls over top of pie before serving.

Yield: 10 to 12 servings

So whatever happened to the fabulous Everleigh Sisters? After the club was shut down by Captain McWeeny, Minna and Aida went to Europe for six months, hoping for the new red-hot reform craze to cool down. (It didn't!) On returning, the sisters opened up a new club on Chicago's fashionable West Side, but the neighbors and the reformers howled. The Everleighs could tolerate the howling, but what they couldn't stand was the 100 percent increase in payoffs that the authorities demanded.

Without further urging they got out of town, taking along as mementos of Chicago Aida's beloved gold-plated piano, Minna's marble-inlaid brass bed, and a few other *objets de coeur*—to say nothing of two million dollars and a cache of precious jewelry.

Through with the bordello business forever, they moved to Manhattan and bought a brownstone (now an apartment house) at 20 West 70th Street, where they lived for thirty years. They resumed the name of their divorced husbands and as Minna and Aida Lester joined several fashionable women's clubs and attended the theater often. Minna died in 1948 at the age of seventy and Aida, bereft of her guiding light, moved to Virginia, where she died in 1960 at age eighty-four.

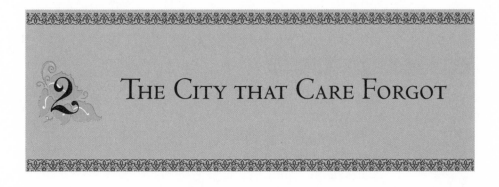

THE CITY THAT CARE FORGOT

New Orleans! Merely breathe the name and the hedonistic juices start jumping. The reflective response to any thought of the city is food, jazz, and flamboyant sex. Food first! People speak reverently of Commander's Palace, of twinkly Paul Prudhomme and his Cajun cookery, of The Morning Call coffee house by the river with *café au lait* and *beignets* any time of the day or night. They sigh in memory of that quaint little oyster bar near the corner of Canal and Royal, the crawfish bisque and *étouffée* all over town and breakfast at Brennan's in the air-conditioned garden (with cocktails, wine, and *café diablo* at 9 A.M.—or earlier).

The city's food triumphs had their origins in the rich mélange of cultures that merged at the mouth of the Mississippi River when New Orleans was still a swamp. The slaves had brought okra from Africa and from that slippery delight came famous Louisiana gumbo, followed by French fried okra served either as a side dish or a lively little cocktail snack. Spices poured in from the West Indies to heat up the local cooking while sorcery with fish and game came in by pirogue from Nova Scotia with the colorful Acadians, now duly famed as Cajuns.

One of the great dishes of the day was brought to New Orleans by a courtesan who had flitted happily through the Court of St. James in the days when heavily upholstered women and corpulent men were fashionable. It is an extravagantly rich concoction that no woman in her right mind would serve more than one or maybe two times a year, but it is so superbly delicious that it deserves a place in your repertoire.

Please do not chicken out and try substituting lighter cream or lower-calorie variants of anything else in the recipe. Let yourself go! Prepare it "as is," enjoy an incomparable dining experience on an ultra-special occasion, and worry about the weight police tomorrow.

Shrimp Mornay

½ cup butter
½ cup flour
½ cup chopped scallions
¼ cup chopped fresh parsley
2 cups heavy cream
1 cup dry white wine
1 teaspoon salt
½ teaspoon white pepper
¼ cup grated Asiago cheese
1 tablespoon lemon juice
Dash hot sauce
1 package (9-ounce) frozen artichoke hearts, thawed
3 pounds shrimp, peeled, cooked and deveined
2 cups sliced fresh mushrooms
¼ cup grated Parmesan cheese

In a medium saucepan, melt butter, stir in flour, and cook over medium heat for 5 minutes, stirring constantly. Add scallions and parsley, cook for 2 minutes, stirring to combine. Slowly add cream, stirring constantly until thickened. Add wine, salt, and pepper, stirring to blend. Add Asiago cheese, lemon juice, and hot sauce, stirring until smooth.

In a 3-quart casserole, alternate layers of shrimp, artichoke hearts, and sliced mushrooms, adding sauce between layers and ending with sauce. Sprinkle top with Parmesan cheese and bake at 350°F. for 30 to 40 minutes, until heated through and the cheese is nicely browned.

Yield: 8 to 10 servings.

Note: This wickedly rich dish calls for a chilled crisp white wine and lots of it.

At the turn of the century, when the city was hitting its stride as the Carousal Capital of the World, the great chefs from France and Spain started coming to town seeking their fortune in the big-spending area that was ingredient heaven. The local waters teemed with fish, shrimp, lobster, crabs, and crawfish; the woods and the bayou swamplands were alive with game, and an abundance of fruits and berries, grains and greens grew in the tropical climate.

The exchange of recipes between the French and Spanish produced the exotic Creole cuisine and when further exchanges were made by the Cajuns, American Indians, blacks, and Latinos the result was the incomparable New Orleans gourmandise.

There are those who feel that the only truly "regional cooking" in the United States is Creole cookery. In fact, Creole cooking is anything but regional. It is not confined geographically to where it originated. It does not rely on indigenous ingredients. Its cuisine relies heavily on a great amalgamation of ingredients that ships brought from every corner of the Earth. Add to that the human element, a wide spectrum of people—blacks, Indians, Spanish, French, British, Germans to name a few. Sound like a gumbo yet?

There is no such thing as an "authentic" gumbo, although there are many dozens that are so called. The word gumbo comes from the African slaves (a derivative of their word for okra), which is why almost every gumbo made contains okra. The recipes that follow have been updated. For instance, they do not use "pure lard" or "knuckle of veal" or call for "simmering on the back of the range for six hours or more."

Note: Most recipes of the times call for serving gumbo with "dry rice, served in a separate dish." However, most modern recipes merely call for serving gumbo over rice—(the rice of your choice). To our tastes, the following recipes produce the best gumbo in New Orleans, which means, simply, that it is the best gumbo in the world.

Shrimp and Crabmeat Gumbo

Originally filé powder (ground sassafras leaves) was the thickening agent for gumbo, a discovery of the Choctaw Indians. Only okra thickens this version.

¾ cup vegetable oil
¾ cup flour
2 cups chopped onion
2 cups chopped green pepper
1 cup chopped celery
¼ cup chopped fresh parsley
2 cloves garlic, minced
1 pound hot smoked sausage, cut into thin slices
1 pound okra, sliced into ¼-inch slices
2 quarts chicken broth
2 cups chopped peeled tomatoes
1 bay leaf
2 tablespoons Worcestershire sauce
1 teaspoon cayenne pepper
Salt and pepper to taste
1 pound raw shrimp, peeled and deveined
1 pound fresh crabmeat, drained and flaked
1 pound fresh oysters, shucked but undrained

THE Bordello Cookbook

In a large Dutch oven, combine oil and flour and cook over low heat, stirring constantly, until the resulting *roux* is dark brown, about 15 minutes. Add onion, pepper, celery, parsley and garlic; reduce heat, cover, and cook about 30 minutes, stirring occasionally, or until vegetables are tender. Set aside.

In a large skillet, cook sausages over medium heat until browned; add sausage to ingredients in Dutch oven. Leave about ¼ cup sausage drippings in skillet and use to sauté okra over low heat until lightly browned. Add okra to Dutch oven, stirring well. Add chicken broth, tomatoes, bay leaf, Worcestershire sauce, cayenne pepper, and salt and pepper to Dutch oven, stirring well. Cover, reduce heat, and simmer for about 2 hours, stirring occasionally.

Add shrimp, crabmeat, and oysters to the Dutch oven, stirring to combine. Cover and simmer for about 15 minutes, or until shrimp turn pink and oysters begin to curl around the edges. Season to taste with additional Worchestershire, cayenne, and salt and pepper.

Yield: 10 to 12 servings

Vegetarian Gumbo

It is said that vegetarian gumbo was common in New Orleans on certain holidays, such as Maundy Thursday. Many vegetables and herbs provided the flavor and the only essential ingredient was okra. The remaining ingredients were left to the imagination of the cook who tossed in any other vegetables at hand, including leftovers. Some interesting lore about vegetarian gumbo includes one secret ingredient, a cup of strong coffee added just at the end, for color and flavor. Another whole clan of cooks always used seven greens for the gumbo—for good luck, of course.

As for jazz, the signature music of the city may or may not have been born there (Chicago, San Francisco, Paris, and the Mississippi Delta all have claimed it). But jazz undeniably grew up in New Orleans, hotly cradled in the wide open bordellos of the red-light district, where song and dance shared feature billing with sex.

When Miss Lulu White came undulating down the staircase in fabled Mahogany Hall, singing her grand entrance song, the blaze of diamonds that came with her could have cracked a glass eye. Her song always was "Where the Moon Shines" and the moon, in full autumnal tumescence, had nothing on Miss Lulu. The madam believed in the friendship of diamonds and her person was paved with her faith.

Miss Lulu flashed diamond rings on every finger, thumbs included. Diamond bracelets marched all the way up to both armpits. A diamond necklace dramatized the overblown décolletage of her glitzy ball gown. A diamond tiara topped her flaming red wig. And, as a change of pace, an alligator brooch sprawled across her bosom in a wicked green fire of emeralds. Eclipsing it all was the celebrated diamond-studded smile, her signal to the local dental college that bridgework doesn't have to be boring.

Gumbo Version II

¾ cup oil
¾ cup flour
1 cut-up capon
1 cup ham chunks
1 cup chopped celery
¼ cup chopped parsley
2 cloves garlic, minced
2 cups peeled, chopped tomatoes
1 quart water
1 chopped onion
½ pound okra
Salt and pepper to taste
1 teaspoon cayenne pepper

Make a dark *roux* by cooking the oil and flour together, stirring constantly for about 15 minutes. Add cut-up capon, onion, celery and garlic to the *roux* and cook over medium heat until vegetables are tender and the capon is brown. Add 1 quart of water, cover, and simmer for about 2 hours. Use this liquid for stock, adding okra, tomatoes, and seasonings. Cover and simmer until okra is cooked through. Taste to correct seasonings.

Yield: 8 to 10 servings

Lulu White was owner and operator of Mahogany Hall, the opulent "entertainment center" at 235 Basin Street in New Orleans. Much of the world still dances to her tune, "The Mahogany Hall

Stomp," a tribute written by her nephew, Spencer Williams, who had been adopted by Lulu at the death of his mother. A lifelong music buff, Lulu encouraged and promoted Spencer's talent, which also produced the immortal "Basin Street Blues." His "Mahogany Hall Stomp," inspired by the hymn, "Bye and Bye," was recorded by many jazz greats of the era, including Louis Armstrong. The famous Satchmo recording of it remains a collector's classic.

Lulu's diamonds were the requisite pledges of friendship from a succession of affluent johns and their additional largesse is said to have underwritten the construction of her outrageously expensive Mahogany Hall showplace. Since no woman at the turn of the century could have borrowed money to build so much as a chicken coop, their gifts were fortunate indeed.

Miss Lulu had magnetic attraction for men and money, although many people who knew her shook their heads and declared that they could never see why. Without the jewelry, she was nondescript—short, stubby, fat—forced to compensate for her lack of beauty with unabashed showmanship. Nobody witnessing the spectacle on stage could have guessed that she had grown up at the business end of a hoe or a gunny sack, chopping weeds and picking cotton. Lulu White, in truth, was an Alabama octoroon who at age eighteen put the cotton fields of Selma behind her and struck out to make her fortune in New Orleans—bringing some classic down-home recipes with her.

Hoppin' John Vinaigrette

Black-eyed peas (Vigna Uniquiculata), the legume of many names (cowpeas, black-eyed beans, field peas, to name just a few), originated in Asia and came to our shores through the slave trade. Hoppin' John is a dish hugely enjoyed by Southerners who consider it mandatory on New Year's Day, when it is eaten to ensure good luck throughout the coming year. It was a favorite of Miss Lulu and the following version has been updated for today's more sophisticated tastes. Serve at room temperature as a side dish.

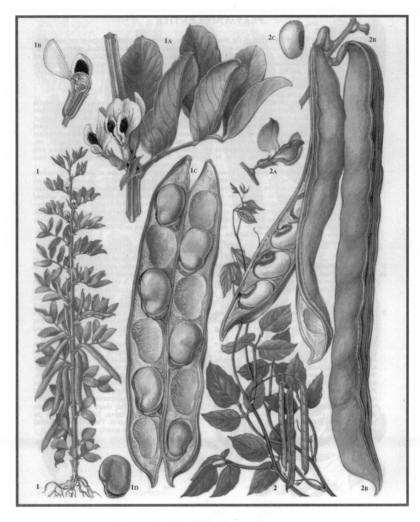

1 pound dried black-eyed peas
8 cups water
1 bay leaf
½ cup chopped red onion
½ cup finely chopped fresh parsley
1 clove garlic, minced
²/₃ cup olive oil
1 tablespoon Dijon-style mustard
¼ cup wine vinegar
Hot sauce (2 or 3 dashes depending on the desired heat)
Salt and pepper to taste

Place black-eyed peas, water, and bay leaf in a large kettle, bring to a boil, reduce heat, and simmer, uncovered, until peas are tender, about 1 hour. Drain, remove bay leaf, and cool.

Place cooled peas in a large bowl. Add onion, parsley, and garlic, and toss to combine.

In a small bowl, combine olive oil, mustard, vinegar, hot sauce, and salt and pepper. Pour dressing over the pea mixture, and toss to coat evenly with dressing.

Yield: 12 servings

Note: Another bit of food lore: Wrap a dime in foil and "hide" it in the finished dish on New Year's Day. The person who discovers the coin in his or her portion gets extra good luck.

Miss Lulu arrived in New Orleans in the 1880s accompanied by a very dark Negro, identified vaguely as her stepfather. Octoroons (persons with one-eighth black ancestry) were looked upon at the time as exotic and in the free and easy underside of the city were extremely popular. Dark Negroes were not.

The black stepfather quickly disappeared and Lulu launched herself into a dazzling career of vice as a "West Indian octoroon." She denied her Alabama heritage, insisting that she was a native of the West Indies "without a drop of Negro blood" in her veins. She was an immediate success, making capital of the prevailing impression that the blending of bloodlines—Negroid or otherwise—produced extraordinary sexual proclivities.

By the turn of the century, Lulu White was the self-declared Empress of the Demimonde. Contrarily enough, so was Josie Arlington, who owned and operated the elite "house of joy" at 225 Basin Street, just a few doors down the block from Mahogany Hall. Both madams advertised themselves as the supreme royalty of their trade. It should be observed, however, that bellicose Josie, described as one of the most battling bawds in town, could never have made it through the door at sedate palaces like the Everleigh Club in Chicago. The elegant Everleigh sisters would have been shocked and mortified at the fistfight Josie got into with a competing black harlot named Beulah Ripley. Beulah tore out most of Empress Josie's hair and Josie, in retribution straight out of the Old Testament, bit off half of Beulah's ear and most of her lower lip. So much for dignity and decorum in New Orleans.

Clearly, madams Arlington and White needed no approval from Chicago in "the city that care forgot." New Orleans was and is unique. It has always had its own arcane attitudes about everything, especially sex, and in Lulu White's heyday went so far as to decriminalize prostitution. In 1898 the whorehouses operating all over town were relocated by city ordinance to a thirty-nine-block area at the edge of the French Quarter. This was the notorious red-light district, bounded by St. Louis, Claiborne, Bienville, and Basin streets. Although prostitution was not officially legalized there, it was officially tolerated. The ordinance defining the district was simply meant to contain and regulate the industry. All previous efforts to deter it had been winked at or laughed out of town.

Once the ordinance was passed, there was a tacit understanding that the entire district was a wide-open marketing ground for ladies of the evening, and those who dared practice their profession in any other area of the city were subject to arrest and fine or jail. Although the vice was not exactly legal in the defined thirty-nine blocks, it was illegal everywhere else.

The decriminalized district was the inspired creation of Alderman Sidney Story, a man of high principles and sincere social conscience. Story despised prostitution. He also loathed jazz, the profession's endemic music, whose very name had a sexual connotation. (In the street language of the time, it had the same meaning as the four-letter word for sexual intercourse.) Jazz was developed and refined by such giants as Louis Armstrong, King Oliver, Tony Jackson, Clarence Williams, and Jelly Roll Morton, all of whom were headline entertainers from time to time in the local pleasure palaces. Morton insisted all his life that he personally invented the jazz medium, much to the annoyance of the others who reluctantly acknowledged his talent

but denounced him as a blow-hard with an irritating habit of denying his black origin.

Never mind where jazz was born. Alderman Story wanted it stamped out along with the prostitution that glorified it. It was he who persuaded the city to pass the ordinance that contained the sex trade within the thirty-nine-block area. And from January 1, 1898, till November 12, 1917, his ordinance stuck. It was his earnest belief that restricting prostitution to that locale would be a deterrent to practitioners and customers alike. He convincingly argued that this containment would check the spread of venereal disease, get rid of pimps and protectors of prostitutes, and allow the city to register brothels for the collection of large tax revenues from their owners. He further declared that it would "remove all cancer of immorality from the view of decent women." Poor Sidney Story. He devoted his life to a heart-rending battle meant to stamp out the sex business and jazz—only to have the whores and happy horn-blowers memorialize him by naming the red-light district in his honor. To his lasting humiliation, it was (and still is) called Storyville.

THE BORDELLO COOKBOOK

The lid was off and the race was on to build grander and grander pleasure houses. Lulu White's Mahogany Hall was a four-story marble edifice constructed at a cost of $40,000, which in today's money would easily top the half million mark.

Just as glitzy as the Hall was Miss Lulu's famous food, which was enjoyed by only a favored few. High on the list of favorites was a Sunday morning breakfast treat called "calas." Made with cooked rice, calas were deep fried and sprinkled with powdered sugar. They were sold by street vendors in the French Quarter, but word had it that the best ones were available at Lulu's.

Calas Tout Chaud

1 package active dry yeast
½ cup warm water
1½ cups cooked rice, at room temperature
3 eggs, beaten
1 cup flour
1 tablespoon sugar
½ teaspoon salt
$1/8$ teaspoon ground nutmeg
Oil for deep frying
Powdered sugar

In a large bowl, soften yeast in warm water. Add rice, mixing well. Cover and let rise in a warm place until double (2 to 3 hours). Beat in eggs, flour, sugar, salt, and nutmeg; cover and let stand in a warm place for about 30 minutes.

In a large skillet, heat 2 inches of oil until hot. Drop dough by the tablespoon into the hot oil and fry until golden brown, turning just once. Drain on paper towels. Serve sprinkled with powdered sugar.

Yield: 3 dozen

Faux Absinthe Cocktail

To accompany the calas, Lulu served strong New Orleans-style coffee and an absinthe cocktail. (Absinthe, a green cordial made from wormwood, with a proof of over 130, was banned in the United States in 1912.) The cocktail can be approximated using any anise-flavored liqueur. Give it a try!

1½ ounces Pernod
¾ ounce water
¼ ounce anisette
Dash of orange bitters

Shake all the ingredients together well with cracked ice and strain into a cocktail glass.

Yield: 1 cocktail

Rivaling Mahogany Hall in baroque splendor was Josie's elaborate playhouse, The Arlington, also a four-story structure, whose embellishments included a new point of interest on the low-slung New Orleans skyline, a Byzantine cupola.

The two houses, only a few doors apart, were monuments to excruciatingly bad taste. Their interiors were much alike, with a "Hall of Mirrors," a profusion of velvet, swagged draperies, bloated Victorian sofas and chairs, teardrop chandeliers, faux Oriental carpets, and erotic paintings and sculptures.

The Arlington boasted a Japanese parlor, the obligatory Turkish parlor, a Vienna parlor, an American parlor, and a number of luxury "dens" and "boudoirs." Mahogany Hall was graced with a broad, spiral staircase designed especially for Miss Lulu's nightly grand entrance. The hall, too, had themed rooms and discreet hideaways for men who demanded discretion or secrecy. But for Miss Lulu, the triumphant feature of Mahogany Hall was the fan window over the doorway—a flashy arc of imitation stained glass with her name and street number spelled out in glittering baubles.

The window, one of the few remaining relics of the notorious house, is now a prized possession of clarinetist Pete Fountain, a contemporary fixture in the area that once was Storyville. Fountain, as this is written, is a headliner at one of the famous hotels along the riverfront. Another Mahogany Hall showpiece, an ornate brass and milk-glass chandelier, hangs in Modell's Restoration and Polishing shop at 4600 Magazine Street. It is tentatively priced at $100,000, although people who know the capricious Ms. Modell strongly doubt that she would sell it at any price.

It is estimated that there were never fewer than five hundred houses of prostitution in the red-light district during its thirty-year existence. Those ranged in size and ambiance from one-woman "cribs" to large, elaborate establishments such as Miss Lulu's and Josie's, each offering the favors of as many as thirty girls.

A grand concoction called dirty rice was invented in Storyville and remains popular throughout the South, particularly in New Orleans. It is divine as a side dish with meat, poultry, or fish.

Dirty Rice

½ cup vegetable oil
3 tablespoons flour
1 cup chopped onion
1½ pounds chopped chicken livers
½ cup chopped celery
½ cup chopped fresh parsley
½ cup chopped green pepper
1 clove garlic, minced
1 tablespoon Worcestershire sauce
Dash of hot sauce
½ cup dry white wine
4 cups cooked rice
Salt and pepper to taste

In a Dutch oven, heat oil, add flour and cook over medium heat to make a roux. Add chopped onions and continue to cook until mixture is brown. Add chicken livers, celery, parsley, green pepper, garlic, Worcestershire sauce, and hot sauce. Cook for a few minutes, stirring constantly. Add wine and cook for an additional 15 minutes. Fold cooked rice into vegetable mixture, and season with salt and pepper. Heat through in a 350°F. oven for about 15 to 20 minutes.

Yield: 8 servings

Note: New-age Southerners top this dish with a sprinkling of Parmesan cheese. Those who don't like chicken livers substitute ham chunks or ground meat that has been lightly browned and often serve it as a main dish.

In upscale whoredom the only serious competition Lulu and Josie had was Countess Willie V. Piazza. Willie was no more a countess than Lulu was a West Indian but her theatrical affinities gave the title an authentic ring. In addition to the monocle she always wore, her props included a two-foot-long ivory cigarette holder and a forty-inch black midget, General Jack Jackson, who served as her doorman. Jelly Roll Morton said he always enjoyed playing at Countess Piazza's place because she was "the only madam in town with sense enough to keep her piano tuned."

Countess Piazza's ménage was made up of a dozen girls widely touted as the most gorgeous octoroons on the continent. Every year on opening day at the Fair Grounds race track, Countess Piazza paraded her spectacular fillies into the high-priced seats—and the respectable ladies of the Garden District filed in right behind them, with their dressmakers in tow to take notes. The countess and her extraordinary octoroons were always dressed in the newest finery from Paris, and the proper matrons—who could not have cared less about horse races—were edified and delighted by the fashion show.

For all their chic, the Piazza octoroons would have been no more likely to pass muster at the refined Everleigh Club in Chicago than bellicose Josie. One amusing story has it that a visitor from Paris appeared at Piazza's house one evening when the countess was out and the woman who Willie had left in charge was unable to communicate with the customer because he did not speak English. The countess was fluent in seven or eight languages but her surrogate, baffled by the Parisian's questions, shouted upstairs; "Does anybody up there speak French?" Back came the loud reply from one of the jaded company: "Good God, do we have to speak it, too?"

Willie Piazza not only spoke French but cooked it superbly. Her cuisine was extraordinary even in New Orleans and her table was another reason why the top girls of the trade gravitated to her jewel-box establishment. Her elegant little candlelight dinners usually ended with a fantastic dessert like this updated sweet.

Chocolate Rum Soufflé

12 almond macaroons
½ cup dark rum (cognac may be substituted)
16 ounces German semi-sweet chocolate, chopped
¾ cup water
½ cup sugar
6 eggs, separated

24 ladyfingers, split
1 cup whipping cream, whipped
Grated white chocolate, for garnish
Candied violets, for garnish

In a shallow wide dish arrange macaroons in a single layer, and sprinkle with rum; set aside. In a double boiler, melt chocolate with water and all but 1 tablespoon sugar, stirring constantly. Remove from the heat and add egg yolks, one at a time, beating well after each addition. Set aside to cool. In a large bowl, beat egg whites with the remaining tablespoon sugar until stiff. Carefully fold beaten whites into the cooled chocolate mixture.

Line the bottom and sides of an 8-inch springform pan with split ladyfingers. Add half the chocolate mixture; top with a layer of soaked macaroons. Add remaining chocolate mixture; top with lady fingers. Cover and refrigerate overnight.

To serve, unmold soufflé, top with whipped cream and garnish with white chocolate curls and candied violets. In a word, WOW!

Yield: 12 servings

The fascination that the demimonde held for ladies of the New Orleans social register was by no means confined to opening day at the racetrack. They listened to any gossipy tidbit they could pick up about the shady ladies and their curiosity set them up for a Mardi Gras caper that neither they nor the demimonde ever forgot.

It came about because madams of the better Storyville houses and their more talented girls were honored every year at a colorful extravaganza called The Ball of the Two Well-Known Gentlemen. Admission to it became a hot ticket and the New Orleans debutantes, present and past, nagged their men from one Mardi Gras to the next to get them tickets to the raunchy event. Although the debs wouldn't dare venture into Storyville any other time, they burned to know what went on there all the time and this was a once-a-year chance to see the naughty girls who regaled their men year round. Once there, safely masked, they could observe the whores at play and afterwards they could dine out for months on stories of the risqué adventure.

It was not to be. When Josie Arlington got word that a group of debutantes would be at the ball, she was incensed. This condescending invasion of a demimonde ball by denizens of respectable society was too much for a proud madam and she promptly made a deal with some friendly policemen. She persuaded them to raid the ball and arrest any woman who did not carry a card registering her as a prostitute in good standing. And so it happened that at the 1906 ball staged by Josie and her friends a number of young ladies representing the cream of New Orleans society were unceremoniously jugged. When they were unable to present the requisite prostitute's credentials they were spirited off to jail where they were unmasked and sent home with an altogether different kind of story to tell their friends.

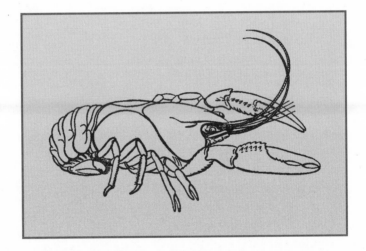

If jazz was the signature music of Storyville, the signature food was crawfish *étouffée*. Crawfish, also known as crayfish, craw dads and crawdaddies, were discovered in the bayou backwaters by the Cajuns. They were at first dismissed as "poor folks food" and spurned by the elite of New Orleans. No self-respecting restaurant would have condescended to put them on the menu until after World War II, when the sophisticated palates of the city began to appreciate these long-neglected country cousins of shrimp. Today the grand chefs of the city outdo themselves and each other in creating new crawfish recipes, and nearly every chic restaurant in town offers a tantalizing version of crawfish *étouffée*.

Shrimp Étouffée

Étouffée is derived from the French and refers to a braised dish. We love it with the crawfish that inspired it but because shrimp is more readily available everywhere (crawfish is abundant only in Louisiana) we offer the recipe that follows. Please don't think of it as a substitute for "the real thing" (crawfish) or as second best in any way. Shrimp *étouffée* is on the menu in the top New Orleans restaurants and we present this recipe as a proud "first."

½ cup butter
1 cup chopped onions
1 cup chopped green peppers
½ cup chopped shallots
2 cloves garlic, minced
1 teaspoon salt
½ teaspoon black pepper
½ teaspoon red pepper
½ teaspoon white pepper
3 pounds large raw shrimp
1 cup chopped scallions
½ cup chopped fresh parsley
Cooked rice

In a large kettle or Dutch oven, melt butter, and add onions, green peppers, shallots, and garlic. Sauté, stirring often, for 30 minutes, or until vegetables are very soft. Add seasonings.

Peel and devein shrimp; place peels (and heads, if shrimp are whole) in a medium saucepan, cover with water, and simmer for 30 to 45 minutes to make a shrimp stock. Strain stock, discarding shrimp shells.

Add shrimp to the vegetable mixture along with enough shrimp stock to cover. Cover the pan and bring to a boil; remove lid and cook, uncovered, for 5 minutes; add scallions and parsley and cook another 1 to 2 minutes, or until shrimp turn pink. Serve over or alongside rice.

Yield: 6 servings

In addition to the practicing prostitutes, madams, pimps, and jazzmen, Storyville was populated with other colorful characters. One was a grotesque little man who walked like a duck, waddling along under a huge, hydrocephalic head and speaking in a strange squiggly voice. He was Ernest J. "Papa" Bellocq, a photographer of remarkable artistry who spent his time and talent among whores and other outcasts, possibly because (like Toulouse-Lautrec) his physical deformity made him feel more at home among obvious social misfits. The few Bellocq photographs that survive reveal a remarkable talent. Many of his glass-plate negatives were defaced by his brother, a Roman Catholic priest, who for reasons yet unknown, stopped short of destroying the plates entirely. Bellocq's work was celebrated in the film *Pretty Baby* starring Keith Carradine, Susan Sarandon, and Brooke Shields. His deformity was ignored in the casting of tall, handsome Carradine to play the Bellocq role—*sans* hydrocephalic head, duck waddle, and squiggly voice.

Another Storyville star was Julia Jackson, the voodoo woman revered and dreaded by the ladies of the evening who were her constant customers.

Voodoo was the avowed religion of Storyville with a following whose disciples believed absolutely in its force. Julia was a six-foot-tall woman of fierce visage. She was seriously cross-eyed, further proof to her naive devotees that she had powers from the world beyond. One of the most feared and talked about was the so-called "sealing power," a curse that purported to "close up" a whore, putting her out of business forever. In *Storyville, New Orleans*, Al Rose reports that the worst threat one whore could make to another was the announcement that she was going to pay Julia Jackson to seal her up. Julia was also reported capable of infecting people with venereal diseases from a distance and it was even believed that she could induce spontaneous abortions and pregnancies. When a defective baby was born in Storyville, the infant was declared fatherless, the product of a Julia Jackson curse.

There were many other voodoo women in Storyville, including Eulalie Echo, the godmother of Jelly Roll Morton. Morton attributed much of the misfortune that dogged him at the end of his life to seances of Eulalie's that he had attended in his youth. But the acknowledged voodoo queen was Marie Laveau who remained a devout Roman Catholic in spite of her cultish carryings on. In her sixties and beyond sexual performing herself, Marie sat in a rocking chair counting her beads while watching over the lascivious pagan rites that she commanded. Laveau ceremonies were attended largely by young white men who came to her ceremonies on St. Ann Street knowing that the voodoo hocus would give way in an hour or so to a sexual orgy of total abandon.

Cream of Artichoke Soup

Many New Orleans food preparations were reputed to "cast a spell" and hot arguments erupted over which were best. Artichokes were declared aphrodisiacal and voodoo spell-casters set them outside overnight when the moon was full "to soak up moon magic." The artichokes were then boiled to a pulp and a huge quantity of chopped raw garlic was added to the mashed bottoms. The resulting dish was supposed to be good for everything from getting a husband to getting rid of one.

We have problems with the moon-magic recipe but heartily recommend the following artichoke soup as a husband-getter or a man-pleaser of any marital status. This soup is elegant hot or cold.

4 large artichokes, cooked and cooled
¼ cup butter
½ cup finely chopped onion
½ cup finely chopped celery
¼ cup flour
1 can (2 pints 14 ounces) chicken broth
¼ cup lemon juice
1 bay leaf
¼ teaspoon dried thyme
2 cups light cream
Salt and white pepper to taste
Sliced lemon, optional
Chopped parsley, optional

Scrape artichoke leaves and finely chop bottoms; set aside. In a large saucepan, melt butter, and sauté onions and celery until soft but not browned. Sprinkle in flour and cook for 1 minute, stirring constantly. Add chicken broth, lemon juice, bay leaf, thyme, and artichoke scrapings and chopped bottoms. Cover and simmer for 20 minutes, or until slightly thickened. Purée mixture in a blender until smooth and creamy. Add cream, correct seasonings, and heat or chill depending on whether serving hot or cold. Float a thin lemon slice topped with chopped parsley in each serving as garnish, if desired.

Yield: 8 to 10 servings

In spite of her voodoo queenship, Marie Laveau apparently never lost cachet with the local church hierarchy since she is buried in St. Louis Cemetery No. 1 at the end of Basin Street. Josie Arlington also made it into the hallowed burial ground, where she was laid to rest in an impressive red marble tomb. Josie had it built at a cost of $35,000 during the fit of depression she suffered after a disastrous fire at Arlington Hall. She had narrowly escaped death in the fire and spent the last months of her life brooding about her misfortunes or disturbing the neighbors with loud and violent tantrums.

The mausoleum she commissioned at the time was nonetheless impressive. Standing at the entrance is a statue of a young girl who appears to be knocking at the door. The statue, carved with a masterly hand, was meant to echo Josie's proud declaration that no girl "ever lost her virginity under the Arlington auspices"—in other words, that she never, to her knowledge, hired a virgin.

This brings us around to our New Orleans Virgin Fizz, chaste daughter of the famed New Orleans Gin Fizz, which was invented by a bartender at the Imperial Hotel in the 1880s. Friends who don't drink alcohol but enjoy the cocktail experience will bless you for this.

New Orleans Virgin Fizz

Juice of ½ lemon
Juice of ½ lime
1 tablespoon cream
1 teaspoon powdered sugar
Seltzer
Dash of orange flower water

Combine all ingredients in a cocktail shaker with cracked ice and shake well. Strain into a 12-ounce Tom Collins glass. Fill to top with seltzer. Stir and serve. For those who prefer their cocktails with alcohol add 2 ounces of gin. Either way, virgin or not, it's wonderful.

Yield: 1 serving

Josie's tomb became a tourist attraction and this, in turn, became so distasteful to relatives of the deceased madam that they sold the tomb and buried her in a place that remains secret. If Phillip Lobano was right, they probably deposited what was left of her in an unmarked grave and pocketed a huge profit from their sale of the sybaritic tomb. Lobano, Josie's one-time "sporting man," always resented her gifts to her family and referred to them as "a pack of vultures." As her pimp, he wanted virtually all of her income at his own disposal, but at the time of her death, he had long been out of the pipeline. Josie had thrown Lobano out years before for killing her brother in a family argument. At any rate, her original tomb is now identified as the final resting place of one J.A. Morales, whose name is carved on the front in place of Josie's.

Of all the Storyville royalty, none had a sadder ending than Lulu White. One account has it that she died on a cot in a boxcar en route to her home in Alabama, where she hoped to spend her last days. While this story has been denied as moralistic fiction, it is established fact that she was ripped off for a huge hunk of her fortune by George Killshaw, the "fancy man" who was her live-in pimp, lover, and business adviser for twenty-four years. The stage was set for his defection when Miss Lulu, sinfully rich and ambitious, cast a wistful eye on Hollywood. It was her plan to become the owner of one of the large film studios—and, perhaps, a movie star! She and Killshaw had made a preliminary foray into the film capital, arriving in a private car with a full complement of costumes, esoteric equipment, and uniformed servants.

Fancy food and elaborate service was, if anything, overdone in the dining room of the pretentious private cars. Menus were pages long, with a sommelier standing by to pour the rarest wines and many a specialty

TYPICAL MENU IN A PRIVATE TRAIN CAR OF THE DAY

Sherried Bouillon
Salt Cod
Pigeons à la Mode
Beefsteaks Cooked with French Turnips
Potted Rabbit
Roast Loin of Veal
Potatoes with Cream
Potatoes à la Maitre de'Hôtel
Calcannon
Stewed Tomatoes
Frenched Green Beans
Salsify
Beaten Biscuits
Harlequin Blancmange
Apple Compote
Chocolate Rum Soufflé
Almond Tart
Coffee/Tea/Beer/Wine/Liqueur

tipple that few of the guests had ever even heard of before. Courses ran into the double digits, with extravagant silver and crystal complementing the food.

Returning to New Orleans, Lulu put the finishing touches on her scheme to buy Hollywood real estate and studio facilities. In January 1907, she sent Killshaw back to California with $150,000 in cash to finalize the deal. But if Killshaw made it to California nobody knew it. He was, in fact, never seen or heard from again. Since he was extremely handsome, charming, and light skinned, it was assumed that he simply took Miss Lulu's money and disappeared into white society where he could easily "pass." The lady suffered but made no effort to locate Killshaw and her cash. She was no sore loser! The next year she built a saloon next door to Mahogany Hall at the corner of Bienville and Basin Street. The building remains standing. She continued to operate Mahogany Hall with declining success until the red-light district was closed down in 1917 by Federal order.

Although Storyville was wiped out, the city still had its food. If it was the incredible madams who made New Orleans the hedonistic capital of the world, they had monumental assistance from the chefs who raised the city's cuisine to Olympian heights.

They, in turn, had help from food-loving cooks and entrepreneurs of every stripe, including the colorful street vendors. It was, in fact, a pushcart peddler who inspired the local rage for oysters by declaring the ugly little mollusks aphrodisiacs. He sold oysters on the half shell, iced and ready to eat out of hand with a special spicy sauce of his own invention. On a slow summer day, he decided to take a shot at boosting business by hand-lettering a discreet sign:

> IMPROVE YOUR LOVE LIFE!
> EAT DELICIOUS
> OYSTERS — 6 FOR 50¢

His stock was a quick sellout, and as word spread a legend was born. Nutrition authorities today say that there was more to his sign than salesmanship, since oysters are a rich source of zinc, and zinc is conducive to sexual health.

Here are two more reasons to love those sexy little oysters!

Corn Oysters

1 cup fresh corn, cut off the cob (or use creamed-style
   canned corn)
1 egg, well beaten
¼ cup flour
Salt and pepper to taste
Dash of hot sauce
1 pint large oysters

In a medium bowl, combine corn, egg, flour, and seasonings. Coat each oyster with a tablespoon of this mixture. Fry in deep fat or cook on a well-greased griddle until golden brown. Turn only once. Serve immediately.

Yield 4 to 6 servings

Curried Oysters

Often served with rice, but for fancy occasions in early New Orleans, patty shells were filled with this luscious curried oyster mixture and garnished with a dollop of chutney.

1 tablespoon butter
1 teaspoon onion juice
1 tablespoon flour
2 teaspoons curry powder
½ cup oyster liquor
½ cup milk
Salt and pepper to taste
1 quart oysters, shucked and drained, reserving liquor

In a small saucepan, melt butter, and add onion juice, flour, and curry powder, stirring to combine. When mixture comes to a boil, add oyster liquor, milk, and seasonings, stirring constantly. When sauce thickens, add oysters and continue to heat until oysters are plump and edges crimp, about 3 to 4 minutes.

Yield: 6 to 8 servings

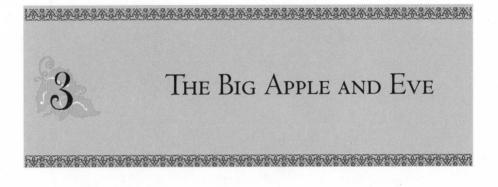

3   THE BIG APPLE AND EVE

"Light ladies" were plying their trade in New York City as early as 1733, the year that Greit Reyneirs, an ambitious barmaid from Amsterdam, hit town. Greit quickly became a role model for her sisters in the trade. With the man she married, a Dutch Moroccan called Turk (because he was born in Fez), she opened a tavern, a handy place to meet potential customers. The potential became actual so quickly that the versatile barmaid had to recruit, and eventually house, a platoon of agreeable girls to help—thus qualifying Greit for a dubious title: First Madam of the Brave New World. Witnessing her easy success at entrepreneurship, other hustlers with no more stake than a month's rent on a few bedrooms began setting up shop as madams and the Big Apple sex business took off.

Bounce, a drink that became popular in colonial times, was "brewed" by pouring a potent drink such as rum over fruit heaped with sugar and letting the mixture ferment. Although New York was not known as "the Big Apple" in Greit Reyneir's time and was, in fact, still New Amsterdam, the apple home brew that inspired this recipe was hugely enjoyed by the colonists. Surprise your friends with this one, for kicks. And we do mean kicks!

Big Apple Bounce

2 quarts sliced cored apples, including peel
1 cup sliced lemons, including peel
2 cups maple sugar
3 sticks whole cinnamon
10 whole cloves
1 quart rum
Water

The Bordello Cookbook

Place all ingredients except water in a large crock or other nonmetallic container and stir to combine. Add enough water to cover fruit. Cover top lightly with a lid or a cloth. Let sit for a week or more at room temperature until the mixture ferments. Strain and serve. Bottle remaining liquor for future use.

Yield: 3 quarts

Note: The fruit bounce was a source of "Dutch courage" for first-timers at Greit's house. (You may, of course, substitute other fruits or berries for apples, if you prefer. Peaches and cherries are especially recommended.)

By 1744, the Battery had become a sexual hotbed (so to speak). Trade was so brisk that Robert Dale Evans, a recorder of the era, estimated that if every prostitute in the area entertained three customers a day, the number of tricks turned each year would top ten million.

In an effort to drive the salesladies out of business, a reformer identified only as the Reverend McDowell diligently collected the names and addresses of all known prostitutes in the Battery and published them in his moralistic *McDowell's Journal*, only to see his well-intentioned publication become treasured as "The Whorehouse Directory." The publication was in big demand by tourists and was sold at a premium by hotel bellboys.

Pot Roast–World's Best and Easiest

Life for the early colonists was a rough and tumble existence and their food was mostly plain and simple fare. Plain and simple would describe most pot roasts. But this recipe may be the one you hand down to future generations as the best pot roast ever—the one that gets raves, the one you never tire of.

1 tablespoon vegetable oil
One 3-pound bottom round beef roast
Salt and pepper to taste
6 cloves garlic, peeled

1 can (1 pound) whole cranberry sauce

In a large Dutch oven, heat oil and brown roast on all sides. Season with salt and pepper. Top roast with garlic cloves and cranberry sauce. Cover and simmer for 2 to 2½ hours, or until roast is fork tender, turning meat occasionally and basting with sauce.

Yield: 10 servings

Note: Serve this pot roast with wide noodles or potatoes. The recipe produces a wonderful sauce and lots of it. The synergy between the garlic and cranberries has an almost sweet-and-sour effect.

In 1836, prostitution became a national *cause célèbre* when the most flamboyant girl in the business was found hacked to death in her bed, with the sheets around her in flames. She was Helen Jewett, known as "the lady in green" because she always wore extravagant green evening gowns as she dined and danced around town in the most fashionable glitter spots.

Helen resided in New York City's most-acclaimed bordello, Madam Rosina Townsend's. Her frequent lover, Richard P. Robinson who was known to have spent at least part of Helen's last evening in her bedroom, was immediately indicted for the murder and, although the evidence against the young man was overwhelming, he was eventually acquitted. The "trash press" had a field day gleefully embellishing every detail of the grisly crime and inventing still other lurid "discoveries," when the case lagged. The Lady in Green became the Green Goddess and her tragic end did little, if anything, to discourage her sisters in vice. Her apotheosis in the press appeared to inspire them and some of them actually seemed to bask in Jewett's reflected glamour.

French Green Pea Soup

Reminiscent in color only of the Lady in Green is this extraordinary soup—an elegant starter for a festive dinner, but so quick and easy you'll be tempted to serve it as a brightener for routine meals.

2 packages (10 ounces each) frozen green peas
¾ cup chopped onion
3 cups chicken broth, divided
Salt and pepper to taste
1 cup light cream
Fresh mint sprigs, for garnish

In a large saucepan, combine peas, chopped onion, and 2 cups of the chicken broth. Cook, partially covered, over medium heat until peas and onion are tender, about 10 minutes. Purée mixture in food processor. Season with salt and pepper. In a large saucepan combine puréed pea mixture with remaining chicken broth and cream. Stir until smooth and of desired consistency. Garnish each serving with a sprig of fresh mint.

Yield: 6 to 8 servings

Note: *This vivid green soup may be served cold, if desired.*

The trade remained rampant, but it was from about 1880 until 1910 that the fabulous parlor houses flourished. A latter-day headliner such as Polly Adler we leave to heaven and history. The earlier madams are, to us, more noteworthy and certainly more fun to write about.

First of all, there was the mystery madam who presided over The Seven Sisters, a row of seven brownstones on West 25th Street between Sixth and Seventh avenues, a richly historic strip that is now a part of the upscale area known as Chelsea. One story about the septet of pleasure palaces has it that a young woman who made a fast fortune running a brothel there persuaded her six sisters to leave their New England hometown and open houses of their own beside hers to share the wealth.

Sister or not, one wily woman was the designated director of the whole conglomerate. Each morning the Managing Madam, whose identity was carefully guarded, made the rounds of hotels favored by titans of industry and politics. She was duly welcomed in the hotel

lobbies by the bell captions, who received frequent queries from their well-heeled (and big-tipping) hotel guests about the available entertainment. The madam left engraved invitations with the captains for proper distribution and her card made it clear that formal wear was *de rigueur* for guests at all of the Seven Sisters.

Champagne, the only alcoholic beverage served, flowed freely at the seven houses, usually with abundant hors d'oeuvres. If a gentleman wanted to dine there, a feast (for two) was ordered in from a nearby restaurant and served at an outrageously marked-up price.

Josephine Wood, an aloof and pretentious loner, was a more than worthy competitor of the Seven Sisters. Her mansion, on Clinton Place west of Broadway, was even more exclusive. A muscular butler stood guard at the carved mahogany and frosted-glass door, admitting only men of immense wealth or exalted political status. To gain admission, even they had to be known to the house or properly recommended. Madam Wood permitted the gentlemen to preview the merchandise, assembling all her available girls in the drawing room where the guests sipped champagne while making their selections from the parade of

THE BORDELLO COOKBOOK

beauties—all luscious but barely literate. (At an average take of $200 per evening, who needed to read and write?)

An added attraction at the Wood establishment was an elegant dinner prepared on the premises every evening by one of the city's premier chefs. The chafing dish had hit its stride in popularity at this time as interest in food moved from the kitchen and family meals to lavish dining and entertaining. New York City was on a roll! Restaurants and hotel dining rooms flourished. Big money was everywhere—flashed nowhere with more aplomb than at Josephine's mansion. An imposing silver chafing dish was always on display there, providing not only a look of elegance but keeping tasty foods warm for an extended period. Who knew when a customer might get a hunger pang? A great favorite was the following "tipsy stew," full of flavor and gusto, just like the state it's named for. It holds well in a chafing dish and can even be reheated should the need arise.

Empire State Stew

2 slices bacon, diced
1 cup chopped onion
1 clove garlic, minced
1 pound lean pork, cut into ½ x 2-inch strips
1 pound lean beef, cut into ½ x 2-inch strips
1 pound lean lamb, cut into ½ x 2-inch strips
2 tablespoons paprika
1 tablespoon caraway seeds
Two (16 ounce each) cans tomatoes
1 cup dry white wine
2 cups julienned leeks
½ cup dry gin
1 cup sour cream
Salt and pepper to taste

In a large Dutch oven, sauté bacon until crisp; remove, add onion and garlic to drippings, and sauté until soft. Remove vegetables, add meat, and sauté until browned. Add vegetables back to the pan along with the paprika, caraway seeds, tomatoes, and white wine; stir to combine, cover, and simmer for 2 hours. Check occasionally to see that the meat is sufficiently covered with liquid; if it seems dry, add ½ cup wine or water. Add leeks, gin, wine and sour cream. Cover and heat through. Do not let boil. Present at the table in a chafing dish. Serve on rice or toast points.

Yield: 10 servings

Note: The chafing dish is really nothing new, going all the way back to Pompeii. It is, however, newly popular among chic hostesses. But if you have a problem keeping food warm you may prefer the electric "hot tray" designed by an enterprising inventor, Lew Salton, back in the '50s. Because he was constantly late to dinner, this easily distracted genius designed it for his wife, and when it was manufactured for general distribution put his name on what the world came to know as the Salton Hot Tray.

The sexual scene in New York was tilted into an uneasy new balance by the arrival of Victoria Woodhull, who blew into town like a cyclone, preaching her three-cornered doctrine of Feminism, Spiritualism, and Free Love. The madams were mystified. This outspoken newcomer was obviously on the side of unrestrained sexual expression. She was also volubly opposed to police harassment of whorehouse keepers, having gone so far as to denounce the cops for their "shakedown" raids on the establishments. Still, the madams and their boarders were stopped cold by the four-letter word no self-respecting pro could abide: "Free." Didn't they have enough amateur competition already without this loud-mouthed advocate of giveaway amour?

While that was not exactly what Victoria Woodhull meant, her fiery but often muddled rhetoric made it difficult for anybody to understand what she did mean. To her, it was no matter because she had something better than public understanding. She had a silver tongue, a poison pen, and the approbation of no less a personage than Commodore Cornelius Vanderbilt, the richest man in America.

According to M. M. Marberry, author of *Vicky, a Biography of Victoria Woodhull*, the Commodore at seventy-six was becoming more and more eccentric. "Grief-stricken after the death of his youngest child, he had taken up Spiritualism, Mesmerism and Clairvoyance, all in tremendous vogue in the 1870s, and had communed with various departed spirits through a variety of mediums."

Vanderbilt was immediately captivated by Victoria and her sister Tennie C. (Tennessee) Claflin who had arrived with her from "somewhere in the Midwest," apparently with pots of money. Together they plunged into the banking business, becoming the city's first lady brokers. Since no woman of the day dared venture into commerce of any kind—let alone banking and brokerage—this was a jolt to everyone but Vanderbilt. The old Commodore was enchanted by their scandalous flouting of the current morals and mores. He enjoyed their "forward" behavior as much as he appreciated their skills at levitation, table-tapping, and summoning up spirits of the departed—the hokum that had attracted him in the first place.

Since the Woodhull-Claflin household was overrun by a weird assortment of dysfunctional family members, radical friends, and live-in servants, the sisters usually ate out. Victoria and Tennessee had leased a mansion at 15 East 38th Street to accommodate this ménage of twenty-four (which included Victoria's first husband as well as her second), but the busy sisters spent little time there. A private table was reserved for them at the Astor and they were regulars also at Delmonico's, Sherry's, and other fashionable restaurants. Marberry observed that "more than once they ordered the breakfast of blades, *pâté de foie gras* and champagne."

Chicken Liver Pâté

The *pâté de foie gras* served back then was a complex concoction requiring twenty or so ingredients and many hours of preparation. Who has the time and patience these days for that? This easy stand-in is a godsend for today's rushed hostess. It's a quick and delicious winner!

¼ cup butter
½ cup finely minced onion
2 cloves garlic, minced
1 teaspoon dried thyme
1 pound chicken livers

1 cup dry white
  wine
¼ cup brandy
½ teaspoon ground
  allspice
1 tablespoon heavy
  cream
Salt and pepper to
  taste

In a medium skillet melt butter, add onion, garlic, and thyme, cover, and cook for 20 to 30 minutes until onion is tender and lightly browned. Add chicken livers and simmer for 10 to 15 minutes (livers should be slightly pink inside).

HOLLANDAISE SAUCE

3 egg yolks, beaten
1 tablespoon lemon juice
½ cup butter, melted
2 tablespoons hot water
Dash of hot sauce

In a double boiler over simmering water, beat egg yolks with a wire whisk until smooth. Add lemon juice and gradually whisk in melted butter, pouring butter in a thin, steady stream. Slowly stir in hot water and hot sauce, continuing to stir for 1 minute. Do not boil. Serve immediately.

Yield: 1 cup

Note: To correct a curdled hollandaise sauce, whisk in a teaspoon of hot water, a drop at a time.

Place liver mixture in food processor, add brandy and allspice, and process until mixture is smooth. Add cream and salt and pepper; process to blend. Transfer to a 2-cup tureen, cover, and refrigerate overnight.

Yield: 2 cups (8 to 10 servings)

Eggs Benedict Manhattan

Many classic dishes that are enjoyed today were created by chefs in the famous hotels of the era and promptly copied in the better bordellos that served meals. It's a toss-up whether eggs Benedict originated at Delmonico's Restaurant or in the Waldorf-Astoria's renowned kitchens, but it is a very New York dish—perfect for a "morning after" brunch or any other meal night or day. Champagne isn't obligatory but it's awfully good with it.

2 English muffins, split
4 slices Canadian bacon
4 eggs
Salt and pepper to taste
Hollandaise Sauce (recipe on preceding page)
Black caviar (just a tiny amount, for garnish)

Toast English muffins, keep warm. Sauté Canadian bacon, place on English muffins, keep warm. Poach eggs by simmering for 3 to 5 minutes or to desired doneness. Remove with a slotted spoon. Season with salt and pepper. Place an egg on top of each slice of Canadian bacon, spoon Hollandaise sauce over all; garnish with caviar. Serve immediately.

Yield: 4 servings

Waldorf Salad

There's no toss-up over the origin of the following perennial. Whatever the hotel chefs used for inspiration it certainly worked because Waldorf salad remains a standard after more than one hundred years. This version picks up new personality from the addition of green grapes and a bit of curry powder.

3 apples
1 tablespoon lemon juice
1 cup chopped celery
½ cup coarsely chopped walnuts
½ cup seedless grapes, halved
½ cup light mayonnaise
½ teaspoon curry powder
Shredded lettuce

Core and quarter apples, leaving the skin on; coarsely chop. Place in a bowl and sprinkle with lemon juice to coat. Add celery, walnuts, and grapes, tossing to combine. In a small bowl, mix together mayonnaise and curry powder; add to apple mixture, mixing well to coat evenly. Serve portions on shredded lettuce or line the serving bowl with lettuce before adding salad.

Yield: 4 servings

Note: Try mixing different kinds of apples, some sweet, some tart. Also you may want to use almond slivers or chopped pecans in place of the walnuts. For best results, be sure the apples you use have a firm texture.

Vichyssoise

Give credit to another hotel chef, this one at the Ritz-Carlton, for the invention of velvety potato-leek soup, served cold. This recipe has fewer calories than the original, plus added zip because it's made with yogurt instead of heavy cream.

Okay, how do you pronounce the name? All together now, say "vihsh-ee-swahz."

2 potatoes, peeled and chopped
4 leeks, well rinsed and sliced
2 stalks celery, sliced
1 can (2 pints, 14 ounces) chicken broth
1 cup plain yogurt
Salt and pepper to taste
Thin lemon slices, for garnish

In a large kettle, combine potatoes, leeks, celery, and chicken broth; simmer over medium heat until vegetables are done, about 30 minutes. Let mixture cool. Purée in a food processor until smooth; add yogurt and seasonings, blending until smooth. Transfer to a bowl, cover, and refrigerate for several hours or overnight. Taste to correct seasonings. Garnish each serving with a lemon slice.

Yield: 6 servings

Variation: For a colorful change, add 1 pound well-rinsed fresh spinach to the vegetables during the last 5 minutes of cooking and add a pinch of nutmeg for garnish to each serving instead of a lemon slice.

Perhaps the best friend the madams had at the century's turn was Diamond Jim Brady whose legendary appetite was echoed by his equally active generosity. He was always good for an emergency loan and when the recipients of his largesse found repayment inconvenient he gracefully tore up their IOUs. Additionally, he was a lavish host whose taste in companionship was by no means restricted to virtue.

In his book called *Diamond Jim, The Life and Times of James Buchanan Brady*, Parker Morrell wrote that wining and dining in those days was an art, considerably enhanced by the elaborate cuisine of the hotels. Fourteen-course dinners were commonplace, always starting with hock (white Rhine wine) and oysters, followed by two soups, clear and thick. Then came the hors d'oeuvres "timbales, palmettes, mouselines, crustades, bouchées and the like." After that was a fish course, "which might consist of terrapin, more oysters, crabs, lobsters, shrimp or frog legs." The roast that followed was often "saddles of lamb, veal, mutton or antelope; or else turkey, goose or capon accompanied by one or two vegetables."

Morrell explained that after the roast there was a respite similar to the half-time at football games. Punch or sherbet was served, supposedly to settle the food that had already been downed and make room for the bounty yet to come. The first course in this second half of the dinner could be venison or antelope if they had not been in the previous parade, and other lavish game dishes consisting of wild duck, goose, grouse, prairie hen, American or English hare, partridge, pheasant, pigeon, and wild turkey or woodcock.

The diners then settled down to hot, sweet dishes of fritters, pudding, pancakes, omelets, or soufflés, then cold sweets such as jellies, creams, blancmanges, and charlottes. Additional dessert courses included assortments of cheese with fruits of every available kind—fresh, dried, preserved, and candied—plus bonbons, ices, ice cream, and fancy cakes.

THE Bordello Cookbook

It was all topped off with French or Turkish coffee, cigars for the gentlemen, and a fine selection of liqueurs for everybody.

Though Diamond Jim drank no alcohol, he saw to it that his guests were served rivers of champagne, Sauternes, sherry, Rhine wine, claret, burgundy, and port throughout the meal, while he drank orange juice—gallons of it! The expansive bon vivant ate meals like the foregoing seven nights a week. He gobbled down three or four helpings of all main dishes in the fourteen-course dinners, finishing, said Morrell, with the greater part of a box of chocolates. He then took along two-pound boxes of candy to eat at the theater, delighting in matching sweets to the fare onstage. He pronounced bonbons best for Shaw and glacéed fruits the ideal accompaniment for Ibsen.

Rum Runner's Rum Balls

Although he had a giant sweet tooth, Diamond Jim could not enjoy the following no-bake sweets because of his well-known distaste for that old devil rum—or, for that matter, anything else containing alcohol. However, he never invoked prohibition on his friends who joyfully drank his share of potables and wolfed down an early version of these.

2 cups graham crackers, crumbled
2 cups powdered sugar, divided
1 cup shredded coconut
2 tablespoons unsweetened cocoa powder
2 tablespoons light corn syrup
½ cup dark rum

In a large bowl, combine all ingredients, including 1 cup of the powdered sugar, mixing well. Shape into firm ¾-inch balls and roll them in a shallow bowl filled with the remaining 1 cup powdered sugar. Store in layers in an airtight container.

Yield: 4 dozen balls

Note: A Southern variation of these sweets calls for vanilla wafer crumbs instead of graham crumbs and substitutes bourbon for rum.

Roast Squab with Tangy Blueberry Glaze

Jim could and did enjoy squab, a premium entrée then and now. It's still very pricey—perhaps more so now—and should it be out of your range, substitute Cornish hen. (No one will know since few people have actually eaten squab.)

2 squab (¾ to 1 pound each), cleaned and trussed
1 tablespoon oil
1 cup dry red wine
¼ cup barbecue sauce
¼ cup blueberry jam
⅓ cup fresh or frozen blueberries, for garnish

In a large skillet, heat oil, and sear squab, turning to brown on all sides. Meanwhile, in a bowl, whisk together wine, barbecue sauce and blueberry jam. Transfer squab to a roasting pan, and brush with sauce. Roast at 425°F., brushing with glaze as needed for 20 to 25 minutes.

To serve, slice breast and fan on plate; place legs and thighs alongside. Garnish with blueberries.

Yield: 2 servings

Note: Squab is very difficult to eat gracefully unless you carve it as described in this recipe. Difficult though it is, squab is considered by many to be the very best fowl.

When Diamond Jim's daily gourmandizing finally overtook him at age fifty-six, his doctors were startled to discover that his stomach was six times as large as normal. Jim was impressed but undeterred. Even at Johns Hopkins Hospital he had his meals sent in from the exclusive Hotel Belvedere. Although he continued to devour incredible quantities of such delicacies as terrapin, roasted meats, game, fowl, and wickedly rich desserts, he was finally well enough to return to his old haunts. He had paid a Baltimore widow $200,000 for the digestive organs of her deceased husband and his enthralled doctors, who often shared his Belvedere meals with him, had prayerfully implanted these in place of his own grossly distorted digestive equipment. He continued to test his new stomach with more relish than restraint until his death in 1917 at sixty-one. According to biographer Morrell, his body lay in state in the living room of his home on 86th Street for two days while hushed and silent crowds came to pay their last respects. The crowd undoubtedly included many a light lady and madam who he had wined and dined and helped through a difficult time with loans for rent or bail money.

Diamond Jim was the larger-than-life icon of a glittering era, a time when eating and drinking were the hallmarks of the good life. The next time you want to give a particularly festive party you might invite special guests to a Diamond Jim dinner with a menu made up of dishes chosen from the bounty listed in the fourteen-course meals described in this chapter. Or, if you're feeling naughty, make it a Seven Sisters party and be sure to state that formal dress is *de rigueur* for the gentlemen, just as the managing madam always stipulated. The ladies may enjoy wearing turn-of-the-century costumes, with lots and lots of rhinestones!

DIXIE DALLIANCE

Atlanta has always been the hub of the South, a flourishing center of commerce even before the Civil War. Although most of it was burned to the ground in Sherman's March to the Sea, the ashes had hardly cooled off before Atlanta was up and running again.

By 1900, the *Gone with the Wind* city was going for broke, already eligible for its current *nom de guerre*, "Hotlanta!" It was the crossroads of the railroads and businessmen from everywhere were in and out, sampling its loudly whispered delights.

Few were more delightful to the cognoscenti than Miss Millie's Gold Rush, a private club accessible only to members in good standing (mostly from the elite of Atlanta) and their discreetly chosen guests. Visitors to the city who were chosen considered themselves signally honored.

As the elegant gentlemen entered Miss Millie's drawing room, each dropped a ten-dollar gold piece into the large crystal goldfish bowl on the marble-topped buffet table. This entitled him to the hospitality of the house—two drinks served by elegantly uniformed blacks, limited socializing with "Georgia's sweetest peaches" (the famous Gold Rush girls), and all he cared to eat from the equally famous Gold Rush buffet.

And what a buffet it was! Georgia was, and is, farm country—a land of mellow loam producing a bounty of the world's great edibles. Miss Millie's buffet was a farmland showcase. There were seasonal variations and daily surprises, but a typical spread included mountains of Southern fried chicken, slabs of sugar-cured smokehouse ham, smothered or barbecued pork chops, fried okra, butter beans, and several other fresh vegetables, potato salad, candied yams, hot biscuits, hot cornbread sticks, homemade fig preserves, pickled peaches, blackberry jam, and quince jelly. That was for starters! The dessert table stood apart and just looking at it was enough to sentence you to six months at hard labor on the fat farm. It was loaded with pecan pie, peach cobbler, banana pudding, chocolate velvet, coconut cream pie, pound cake, and Miss Millie's Special Gold Rush Cake (made with peach conserve).

Since fried chicken was mandatory at Miss Millie's and is undoubtedly the best known and most hotly argued Southern dish of all time, a few more argument starters are in order here. Every southerner alive can attest that the fried chicken of his or her own—or the fried chicken cooked up by Mama, Mama's Mama, or some treasured family cook—is the one and only real thing, just "the absolute best fried chicken you ever put in your whole mouth!"

All right, already! Granted, there are uncounted ways to do fried chicken but we dare to put forth a few rules for Southern fried that we hold to be inviolable. First of all, the chicken parts must be properly disjointed and cut up, not randomly hacked apart. These must be floured and fried in hot fat deep enough to come halfway up the sides of the chicken parts. The oil used is optional but, generally speaking, a solid shortening or vegetable oil is fine. Most Southerners demand a black cast-iron skillet but if you haven't inherited one of those, there are many sturdy fry pans available today that work. Down yonder, they caution *take your time*. Chicken should be fried s-l-o-w-l-y over medium heat as directed in the following recipe.

Another Southern commandment: Thou shalt eat fried chicken only with thy fingers. (And you wondered how "finger lickin' good" came to be used as an advertising slogan?)

THE BORDELLO COOKBOOK

Southern Fried Chicken

2½ to 3 pound chicken, cut up
1 cup milk (or buttermilk)
1 cup flour
Salt and pepper to taste
Vegetable oil or solid shortening

Soak chicken parts in milk for ½ hour. Place flour and salt and pepper in a paper bag; remove chicken from milk and shake in bag with flour mixture until pieces are thoroughly coated.

Heat shortening or oil in a cast-iron skillet (or heavy fry pan). Add several pieces of the chicken, leaving space between the pieces to avoid crowding the pan. Fry over medium heat until chicken is golden brown on one side, about 15 minutes; turn and fry until tender and golden brown all over, about 20 to 30 minutes more. Remove chicken from pan and drain on paper towels. Repeat with remaining chicken parts.

Yield: 6 servings

Southern Barbequed Chicken

As already mentioned, the variations on Southern fried chicken are infinite. Some cooks add cornmeal to the flour or coat the chicken with crushed corn flakes, still others dip it in a batter made of flour, milk, and endless combinations of spices and exotic herbs. These can all be delicious but then the chicken is something else—no longer Southern fried.

Today, probably more Southern chicken is done on the grill. While it is in no way the same as Southern fried, it is embraced as healthier and easier. Barbecue sauces vary even more than the recipes for fried chicken but we include two of our favorites.

2½ to 3 pound chicken, split or quartered
2 tablespoons vegetable oil
2 cups Barbeque Sauce (recipes follow)

Brush chicken with oil, and grill over medium-hot coals until tender and brown, brushing with oil as needed.

BARBECUE SAUCE #1

1 cup ketchup
⅔ cup cider vinegar
⅓ cup brown sugar
¼ cup vegetable oil
¼ cup Worcestershire sauce
2 tablespoons prepared mustard
1 tablespoon smoke-flavored liquid
2 cloves garlic, minced

Combine all ingredients in a small saucepan, stirring to combine. Heat to boiling, reduce heat, and simmer for 10 minutes. Brush on during last 10 minutes of grilling. Pass remaining sauce when chicken is served.

Yield: 2 cups

BARBECUE / MARINADE SAUCE #2

½ cup soy sauce
½ cup tomato juice
½ cup vegetable oil
2 cloves garlic, minced
1 teaspoon grated fresh ginger
1 teaspoon prepared horseradish

Combine all ingredients in a bowl. To use as a marinade, coat chicken with half the mixture and let it stand for 30 to 60 minutes. Use remaining mixture to baste the chicken during grilling.

Yield: 1½ cups

During the last 10 minutes, brush chicken with barbeque sauce. Serve remaining sauce with chicken. It's a marvelous dunk for French fries, too, and a dandy sop for the garlic bread that almost always accompanies a Southern barbeque.

Yield: 6 servings

Down South, no barbecue is declared "respectable" until the cole slaw comes on, and here's one our Georgia friends swear by:

Coleslaw Hotlanta

4 cups finely shredded green cabbage
6 scallions, thinly sliced
1 cup mayonnaise
¼ cup sour cream
¼ cup vinegar
¼ cup sugar
Salt and pepper to taste

In a large bowl, toss together cabbage and scallions to combine. In a small bowl, combine remaining ingredients, stirring until smooth. Pour over cabbage mixture and toss. Cover and refrigerate for at least an hour, or until ready to serve.

Yield: 8 servings

Variations: Add chopped red cabbage, red onions, carrots, celery; 1 teaspoon celery seed or 1 tablespoon prepared mustard.

While club members and their guests ate and drank at the Gold Rush, they enjoyed the company of the young ladies in residence who were not otherwise engaged upstairs. Although most of them had never finished high school, Miss Millie had given all of them a liberal education in Gold Rush banter and was proud that all of them could make even the nerdiest client feel brilliant, witty, and altogether fascinating. When a gentleman wished to take one of Georgia's sweetest peaches upstairs, another trip to the goldfish bowl was in order. He whispered his choice to Miss Millie who delicately negotiated a fee, the amount depending on the popularity of the girl, the services desired,

and the length of time the client expected to spend upstairs. All-nighters paid dearly, but were dearly rewarded with very special treatment. They received, among other extras, a complimentary breakfast preceded by a bracing eye-opener made with store-bought liquor—never the moonshine that sent a whole generation of Georgians into orbit.

Breakfast in the South has nothing to do with the time of day, really. It's more a matter of what you eat when you get up. It could be 6 A.M. or high noon. Coffee is critical. If the evening has been a large one, you might start with a "jolt" of something stronger, usually served in or with the coffee. Hearty breakfasts at the Gold Rush included a

The Bordello Cookbook

variety of dishes considered "stomach settlers"—things like grits, spoon bread, muffins, and biscuits. The following are a few examples but, first, the "jolt."

Plantation Eye Opener

(Have a *real* good morning!)

1 teaspoon good orange marmalade
Pinch fresh nutmeg
¼ cup water
1 jigger whiskey
Cracked ice

Dissolve marmalade and nutmeg in water. Add whiskey and ice and shake well. Serve in an old-fashioned glass and top with another pinch of fresh nutmeg, if desired.

Yield: 1 serving

Basic Grits

1 cup quick grits
4 cups water
½ teaspoon salt
Butter

In a medium saucepan, bring water to a boil, and stir in salt and grits. Reduce heat, cover, and simmer. Stir frequently until grits are thick and creamy, about 5 minutes. Serve topped with butter, if desired.

Yield: 6 servings

Note: If using regular grits, follow same directions but cook for about 40 minutes

Grits / Southern Fried

Cook grits according to package directions or as above. Pour into a 9 x 5-inch loaf pan. Cover and refrigerate several hours. Cut into ½-inch slices and fry on both sides in a small amount of butter (or bacon fat) until golden brown. Top with butter and/or maple syrup, if desired.

Yield: 6 servings

Spoon Bread

2 cups water
1 teaspoon salt
1 cup cornmeal
2 tablespoons butter
4 eggs, beaten well
1 cup buttermilk

In a medium saucepan, bring water with salt to a boil. Add cornmeal in a slow, steady stream, cooking and stirring for about 1 minute. Beat in butter, eggs, and milk until smooth. Pour into a buttered 1½-quart casserole. Bake at 400°F. for about 40 minutes, or until golden. Serve immediately.

Yield: 6 servings

Hominy Muffins

¼ cup hominy
½ cup boiling water
Pinch of salt
1 cup milk, scalded
1 cup cornmeal
¼ cup sugar
¼ cup butter
1 tablespoon baking powder
2 eggs, separated

The Bordello Cookbook

Preheat oven to 400°F.

In a large bowl, combine hominy, boiling water and salt, and let stand for a few minutes to let hominy absorb the water. In separate bowl, mix together scalded milk, cornmeal, sugar, and butter. Combine the two mixtures, add baking powder, and set aside to cool. Beat egg yolks and add to the cooled mixture. Beat egg whites until stiff but not dry; add by thirds to the mixture, gently folding to combine. Line cups of a 12-cup muffin pan with muffin papers and spoon batter into them, filling about two-thirds full. Bake 15 to 20 minutes, or until golden.

Yield: 12 muffins

The girls who roomed at the Gold rush were, by and large, underprivileged young beauties from rural areas of Georgia, Alabama, and Mississippi. Occasionally, Miss Millie took in a girl from Texas but she preferred "home grown talent from closer by—not so inclined to be wild and unruly." Most of her girls had been born and raised on the farm and had fled to Atlanta to escape the drudgery of working in the fields and the boredom of "living in the sticks where nothing ever happens." If any of them felt guilty about what they were doing for a living the guilt was assuaged by their share of the goldfish bowl. All of them were happy to be making more money in one night than they had ever seen before in a whole year. Miss Millie generously split the fees with them on a fifty-fifty basis but charged them a hefty sum for room, board, medical attention, and laundry.

Since the Gold Rush was a private club catering to an upscale clientele, life was high-spirited there but seldom rowdy. A rather jolting crisis arose one night when a guest from Chicago recognized one of Miss Millie's girls as his own niece, the daughter of his sister in Mississippi. He had thought she looked familiar when he first came in but he hadn't seen his niece since he left Mississippi ten years before when she was fifteen years old. Suddenly her identity dawned on him and the shock was electric. Beside himself with confused anger, he promptly threatened to kill Miss Millie for "making a whore out of my only sister's child," then seized the girl's arm and lead her outside to read her the riot act for her disgraceful behavior.

"Lucie Jean," he railed, "How could you do this wicked thing to your mother? My dear sister has worked her fingers to the bone since the day you were born, doing all she could to give you some advantages in life and help you make something of yourself. Your poor mama even picked cotton all day in the blazing sun and then drug herself home to cook supper for you kids and your daddy—"

"I know that, Uncle Ed," she interrupted. "I know it and I appreciate it. That's why I got Mama a job right here in Miss Millie's kitchen, making good money for her cooking, for a change. She's real happy with the set-up. Go ask her!"

Uncle Ed went back into the house, grabbed his hat, and left, without even telling his sister he had enjoyed the buffet.

Braised Pork Down South

Even Uncle Ed might have come back for one of Miss Millie's great pork dishes—like this one that Georgia made famous.

One 3-pound boneless pork loin roast

1 tablespoon olive oil, divided

3 to 5 garlic cloves, peeled

Salt and pepper to taste

½ teaspoon *each* of dried sage, rosemary, and thyme

½ cup dry white wine

½ cup apple juice

24 white tiny boiling onions, peeled with X cut at root end

3 tart green apples, cored and quartered

2 butternut squash, peeled, seeded, and cut into 2-inch
    wedges

¼ cup brandy

1 tablespoon lemon juice

Preheat the oven to 350°F.

Rub the pork roast with half of the olive oil and stud with
garlic cloves. Place remaining oil in a Dutch oven and
brown pork over medium heat until golden on all sides,
turning often. Sprinkle with salt, pepper, sage, rosemary, and
thyme. Add wine and apple juice, cover, and braise for 1
hour.

Boil onions in salted water 5 minutes; drain. Add onions,
apples, and squash to the Dutch oven, placing them evenly
around the roast and basting them with pan juices. Cover
and continue to braise for 1 hour, or until pork is tender.
Transfer pork roast and trimmings to a serving platter.

Skim off layer of fat from the top of the cooking juices.
Place Dutch oven over medium heat and add brandy and

lemon juice, cooking about 3 to 5 minutes to reduce. Adjust seasonings, stirring to blend. Pour reduced pan juices over pork roast and vegetables or serve on the side.

Yield: 6 servings

Potato-Turnip Purée

Here is the perfect complement for rich, savory roast pork. If one root vegetable is good, two are bound to be better. It's an old Southern custom and a good one!

1½ pounds russet potatoes, peeled and cut into 1-inch
   pieces
1½ pounds turnips, peeled and cut into 1-inch pieces
½ cup light cream, warmed
1 tablespoon butter, softened
Salt and pepper to taste

Place potatoes and turnips in a large pan and cover with water. Cover pan and bring to a boil over medium heat; reduce heat and cook until tender. Drain. Rice or mash vegetables, stir in cream, butter, and salt and pepper. Transfer to serving dish.

Yield: 6 servings

Since there are no public records of Miss Millie's Gold Rush, we have relied on stories handed down from customers who gloried in bragging about their good old hell-raising days. The story of Lucie Jean came to us from a young man who said his grandfather swore he was there the night Lucie Jean's uncle recognized her as his sister's wayward child. Apparently, Miss Millie's operation was a well-sealed secret or, at least, a paragon of discretion because the Gold Rush reportedly was in business during the tenure of James L. Beavers, the Atlanta Police Chief whose crackdown on prostitution from 1911 until 1915 reached crusade proportions. Although Miss Millie is not mentioned in public records of the crusade, many another bad housekeeper figured prominently in the reports. Naughty ladies known as Tessie Roulette, Bessie Lamont, Daisey Mobley, and Belle Burton all cropped up often in police and/or press reports.

Chief Beavers's zeal was fueled by an Atlanta organization called the Men and Religion Forward Movement (MRFM), a coalition of reform-minded businessmen determined to stamp out the trade in which many of their business associates had heavy investments. The notoriety of one red-light district was caught by a late nineteenth-century rhymester, like so:

> Peters Street for wagon yards
> Whitehall Street for stores
> Peachtree Street for dressy feet
> And Collins Street for whores.

Champagne Cocktail (Collins Street Special)

A favorite drink in the area was this one and it's easy to account for its popularity. (It's peachy!)

1 ripe Georgia peach, peeled, pitted, and sliced
1 tablespoon lemon juice
Splash of grenadine syrup
1 split dry champagne, chilled

Place peach slices, lemon juice, and grenadine in blender; purée until smooth. Pour mixture into champagne glass, and top with cold champagne, stirring to combine.

Yield: 2 large drinks

Note: To pack a stronger punch, substitute Southern Comfort for grenadine and watch out!

By 1910, the madams had migrated *en masse* from Collins to a rejuvenated strip that had also been rechristened Manhattan Street. The Manhattan migration had been touched off by Charles Jones, an Atlanta entrepreneur who owned the Rex Saloon and had various stakes in horse racing. Jones had face-lifted the cheerless street by building four impressive mansions and stocking them with an assortment of belle-quality girls. The district quickly became known as The Tenderloin—and was, naturally, the number one target of Chief Beavers when he took over the police department.

Which reminds us that when Southerners want to impress company at mealtime, the choice is clear. It's beef tenderloin. Never mind that the word "tenderloin" had another connotation, inspired by the areas where the girls were.

Tenderloin Romantique

4- to 6-pound beef tenderloin, trimmed
2 red onions
½ chopped fresh rosemary
½ cup chopped fresh mint
½ cup good bourbon
½ cup tomato juice
½ cup balsamic vinegar
½ cup olive oil
6 to 8 garlic cloves, peeled

Place beef in a large, shallow dish (glass, ceramic, or plastic). Place remaining ingredients in container of food processor, cover, and process until smooth. Pour mixture over beef, cover, and marinate in refrigerator for several hours or overnight.

Preheat the oven to 425°F. Drain beef, reserving the marinade. Place beef on a rack in a roasting pan and roast for 35 to 45 minutes, basting occasionally with reserved marinade until beef is of the desired doneness. Bring remaining marinade to a boil and serve on the side as a sauce.

Yield: 8 to 10 servings

Urged on by the MRFM, Atlanta's top cop—tough, self-righteous, and unrelenting—made a holy war of shutting down prostitution. Finally, in September 1912, Beavers struck with full vengeance. He personally toured all fifty of the recognized "resorts" to announce that at midnight on the following Saturday (less than a week away) they would be officially closed by the police.

According to an article in *Business Atlanta*, written by Nancy Neill, the city was stunned. "Prostitution may have been illegal and even distasteful," she wrote, "but restricted districts had been considered a necessary evil to keep prostitution confined and out of 'respectable' neighborhoods. Since the Civil War, houses of prostitution had not only been tolerated but 'fined' periodically by the city—essentially, a form of licensing."

It was further reported that one of the madams, Nellie Busbee, whose house had been shuttered, staged the ultimate protest by committing suicide, stabbing herself fatally with a pocket knife. *The Atlanta Constitution* added that clenched in the dying Nellie's fist was a note asking "Chief B_____to go to hell."

Chief Beavers was triumphant but his crusade cost him his job. A new mayor who apparently disapproved of the Chief's policies succeeded in getting him tried for incompetency and demoted to captain, whereupon Beavers resigned. Miss Millie evidently survived not only the Beavers crusade but the great Atlanta fire of 1917, which destroyed much of the old Fourth Ward, where the Gold Rush is thought to have been located. The last tales of the goldfish bowl that reached us were set "somewhere in the 1920s" and indicated that Miss Millie remained unsinged.

An article provided by the Atlanta Historical Society states: "There is little written history about prostitution in Atlanta during the early years of city growth. By 1878, the Atlanta City Directory listed at least one madam, Abbie Howard. She appeared in bold, black type indicating that she was a subscriber to the publication. She was listed as a madam, which was abbreviated 'Mad,' residing on Line Street between Pryor and Ivy Streets."

The article also states that Abbie is reportedly a woman of some substance, possibly a prototype of Belle Watling in *Gone with the Wind*.

According to local legend, there really was a Belle Watling in Atlanta, presiding over an uppercrust sex emporium during and after "the unpleasantness between the states—showing no partiality to either side as long as the man at the door had the requisite $3 and behaved himself.

In the great Southern tradition of raconteurs, a prominent Atlanta attorney amused his friends for years with a harmless bit of fiction about his grandfather (also an attorney) having defended the madam's right to hang a sign outside her house—a white shelf with a big, black $3 mark painted on it. The purpose of the sign, he said, was not to advertise her trade but to define her market.

"Belle catered to the nabobs," he explained, "the carriage trade, the Federal officers, carpetbaggers and what was generally known as the folding money boys. She had little tolerance for lint heads, cotton choppers and others in the small change crowd. Her sign was merely meant to separate the sheep from the goats." (Since three dollars then equates with about fifty now, the sheep and the goats were many a pasture apart.)

The storyteller went on to say that Belle's simple $3 sign precipitated a minor Civil War re-run when the solicitor general squared off against the feisty madam, attempting to tear her sign down and declare her manse a nuisance. His grandfather, said he, fought the case right up through the Supreme Court—and won! Belle could now swing her sign in the breeze legally and as a token of her appreciation she gave the raconteur's grandfather a gold watch engraved with a replica of the $3 sign. "Unfortunately," he continued, "my grandmother wouldn't let him carry the watch."

Belle Ringer

> 1 jigger bourbon or rye
> Dash of lemon juice
> Dash of grenadine syrup
> Dash of Benedictine
> Crushed ice
> Maraschino cherry, for garnish

Combine all ingredients in a cocktail shaker, and shake well. Serve in a stemmed glass with the cherry for garnish.

Yield: 1 drink

Vidalia Vamp

We can't leave Georgia without a nod to Vidalia onions, a springtime speciality renowned for sweet and mellow flavor. The name is protected under Georgia law and true Vidalia onions must be grown in specified counties in southeast Georgia near the town of Vidalia, where the heat and humidity are ideal for their cultivation. Here's one of the best ways we know to enjoy them:

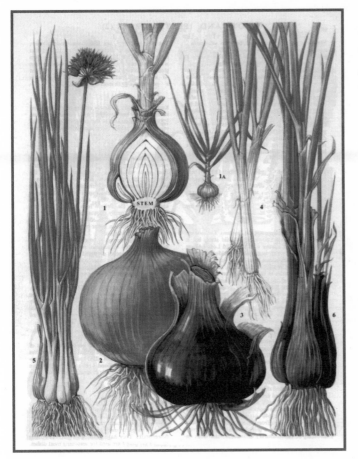

A beguiling side dish for meat or poultry. No substitutes, please. Only genuine Vidalia onions will do!

¼ cup butter
5 Vidalia onions, thinly
  sliced
Salt and pepper to taste
¼ cup dry sherry
Dash of hot sauce
¼ cup grated Parmesan
  cheese

Melt butter in a heavy skillet, add onions, and sauté over medium heat for 6-8 minutes, until tender-crisp. Add remaining ingredients, stirring to combine. Simmer briefly and serve immediately.

Yield: 6 servings

Pride-of-the-South Pecan Pie

Nor can we leave the state without passing along this recipe for the ultimate pecan pie—ultimate *plus* when you make it with genuine Georgia pecans.

Pastry for 9-inch pie shell
½ cup butter, softened
½ cup sugar
¾ cup light corn syrup
¼ cup honey
3 eggs, lightly beaten
1 teaspoon vanilla extract
1 cup chopped pecans
1 cup pecan halves, toasted and lightly salted
Whipped cream, optional

Preheat the oven to 350°F.

In a large bowl, cream butter and sugar with an electric mixer until light; add corn syrup, honey, eggs, and vanilla, beating to combine. Stir in chopped pecans. Pour mixture into prepared pie shell. Arrange pecan halves in concentric circles over top of filling. Bake until top is golden and filling is firm in the center, about 1 hour. Cool. Serve with whipped cream (the weight police aren't watching!).

Yield: 8 to 10 servings

The South has long been peppered with houses of prostitution, many of them one- or two-girl establishments in small towns or nearby rural areas. It was not unusual for these houses to provide room and board for favored guests who came there for an extended stay as a hiatus from family quarrels. When things simmered down at home, the men paid up and went back to the wife and kids. One such house was applauded for serving a "last supper" to departing men who had been in residence for a week or two.

Departing guests were served a meal of their very favorite foods accompanied by their very favorite wines and served, of course, by their very favorite girls. One such fond adieu was made fonder by this menu:

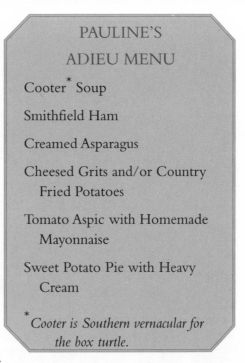

PAULINE'S
ADIEU MENU

Cooter* Soup

Smithfield Ham

Creamed Asparagus

Cheesed Grits and/or Country
  Fried Potatoes

Tomato Aspic with Homemade
  Mayonnaise

Sweet Potato Pie with Heavy
  Cream

* *Cooter is Southern vernacular for
  the box turtle.*

The women who ran these parlor houses excelled in creating a "homey" atmosphere and were often capital cooks, preparing the kind of comfort foods that are still cherished by expatriate Southerners everywhere. The famed House on Clay Street in Bowling Green, Kentucky, was such a place. It was the proud achievement of Pauline Tabor, a former Sunday school teacher who, as the divorced mother of two sons, turned to prostitution as a means of survival—and made a fortune. Although she came to blaspheme "the bible thumpers" of her past, it seems somehow appropriate that a speciality of The House on Clay Street was this former Sunday school teacher's Angel Cake (or angel food cake as it is now called.)

We don't have Pauline's recipes, but this bit of lore about her has been helpful to us in making desserts that are basically simple, yet extremely impressive. Clever woman that she was, Pauline used the whites of her eggs for the cake and the yolks for a custard she served alongside. For special occasions, fresh berries or ripe fruits were used for garnish. And for really special soirees, Pauline made the cake *very tall*, by splitting it horizontally in thirds, piling custard between the layers, then arranging fresh fruits and berries on top. It must have been quite an architectural presentation—the kind currently favored by the leading dessert chefs in New York City, and other food-obsessed cities. Try it with the recipes you have for angel food cake and vanilla or lemon custard.

Pauline took the unusual step of locating her illicit business in her hometown where she was well known as a respectable young matron. Before her divorce, she had belonged to all the right clubs and moved in the favored social circles.

"So why run away to some strange place?" she reasoned, "Why not remain right here where I'd be operating in familiar surroundings and dealing with people I know?" (Naive Pauline! She seemed genuinely surprised when it developed that most of her old friends were no longer able to remember her name.)

Evidently Pauline's veneer of Sunday school respectability masked a tough core—a free spirit underlaid with cast-iron determination. Once she became a madam she enjoyed nothing more than profane and bawdy battle with the town's "holy Joes." She had started out in the business innocently enough, as a reticent and timid freelancer, having found it impossible to make a living at the only job she could get, selling cosmetics door-to-door. A bellman at the local

The Bordello Cookbook

hotel was happy to book dates for her with lonely traveling men and she was happy to pay him a dollar for each booking.

The year was 1933, the bottom of the Depression, and it looked as if the only thing anybody was buying was what Pauline was selling. She began getting more calls from the hotel than she could handle and rather than turn down so much easy money decided to recruit some girls to take care of the overflow on a percentage basis.

Toying with the idea of going into the sex business in a big way, she spent a weekend in the luxurious brothel of "Miss May," a wealthy madam in Clarksville, Tennessee, who enjoyed the friendship (read partnership) of the Clarksville chief of police. She returned home fortified by the advice and encouragement of both the madam and her police chief. Both of them assured her that operating a house of prostitution was in a way honorable, because it was a genuinely needed community service. With any misgivings she might have harbored thus dispelled, she plunged wholeheartedly into her newly chosen profession, determined to operate Bowling Green's "finest house of ill fame." Her ultimate triumph was the house she cherished at 627 Clay Street. In her proud autobiography she declared it "famous for more than twenty-five years as a plush palace of pleasure, providing all manner of gracious loving for well-heeled customers from all parts of the nation."

Pauline was an accomplished cook, who added to the repertoire of her girls by teaching them homey little tricks of the kitchen. The following Clay Kitchen descendant is popular in the South today, served as an hors d'oeuvre or a salad.

Confederate Caviar (Cheap Chic)

This is the kind of recipe that utilizes a basic ingredient (black-eyed peas), lifting it to a new place—a delicious appetizer. It is also used as a salad by several admired hostesses we know.

1 pound dried black-eyed peas, cooked, drained, and cooled
½ cup diced green pepper

½ cup diced red pepper
½ cup diced onion
½ cup finely chopped fresh parsley
½ cup finely chopped carrots
3 cloves garlic, minced
1 jalapeño pepper, minced
1 cup olive oil
⅓ cup white vinegar
1 tablespoon Worcestershire sauce
Salt and pepper to taste

In a large bowl, combine black-eyed peas with green and red peppers, onion, parsley, carrots, garlic, and jalapeño pepper. In another bowl, whisk together remaining ingredients; pour over the pea mixture, tossing to combine. Cover and refrigerate for several hours or overnight. Serve with crackers or tortilla chips as an hors d'oeuvre, or on lettuce as a surprise salad.

Yield: 8 cups

In that all-too-candid autobiography, Pauline Tabor gives us a look at Christmas in the whorehouse, which is something we had never thought about before but have brooded about since. "Christmas in most brothels is strictly Dullsville," says she, "A time when most tricks are abstaining from pleasures of the flesh because of the holy season, too busily engaged with their families or too broke from the rigors of holiday shopping. On the other side of the street, most girls are given the holidays off to spend Christmas and New Year's with their families. This leaves most houses with just a skeleton staff: the madam, a few girls who have no family to celebrate with, and a few part-time prostitutes seeking to bolster their holiday budgets by helping to handle the tricks who like some extra frills added to the mistletoe routine."

Because most Southern ladies "put up" fruit during the high fruit season, fabulous fruit dishes were available throughout the year and were on the menu often. This one could brighten up any meal that needs a shining finish.

Brandied Peach and Berry Cobbler

3 cups peeled and sliced peaches
1 cup berries (preferably boysenberries)
¼ cup brandy
6 tablespoons cornstarch
½ cup brown sugar
2 cups oatmeal
½ cup cold butter, cut into pieces
1 teaspoon baking powder
1 teaspoon ground cinnamon
½ cup buttermilk
Juice and grated zest of 1 lemon

In a large bowl, combine peaches, berries, brandy, cornstarch, and brown sugar; let stand for 15 to 20 minutes. In a food processor, combine oatmeal, butter, baking powder, and cinnamon; process, using quick on-and-off motions until the mixture resembles coarse meal. Add buttermilk, lemon juice, and lemon zest, process until smooth.

Preheat the oven to 350°F.

Stir fruit mixture to combine, and spoon into a buttered 2-quart casserole. Drop dough from a tablespoon on top of fruit, spacing evenly. Bake for 30 minutes, until lightly browned and bubbly. Cool to room temperature. Serve topped with vanilla ice cream, if desired.

Yield: 8 servings

Pauline delighted in telling about the tradition at her house of cheering up the season by adopting a needy family. The first time they did this they had volunteered to take part in the local newspaper's annual Adopt-a-Family drive, only to find the editor reluctant "to accept charity from a whorehouse." He gave in only after Pauline threatened to start a drive of her own that would eclipse the newspaper's. The editor retaliated by giving Pauline and her girls one of the toughest, most expensive cases in town. He assigned them a large

Negro family on the brink of starvation—a mother, father, and twelve children, ranging in age from seventeen to seven months.

The House on Clay Street went into action. Not waiting until Christmas, they immediately sent tons of coal to the heatless house plus blankets, furniture, and emergency supplies of food and clothing. For Christmas Day, they amassed a huge collection of toys and spent hours baking turkeys, ham, cookies, and other holiday goodies, then recruited a fat fireman to accompany them to their adopted family as Santa Claus. No needy case in the history of the newspaper's drive had ever experienced such a sumptuous Christmas! Although the reluctant editor recognized the element of spite in Pauline's largesse, he realized that it matched his own spite in assigning her such a tough case in the first place and warmly welcomed her participation thereafter.

This, of course, brings us around to a very old Southern custom:

Christmas Turkey

Christmas turkey was, and is, a holiday tradition in the South. The fact that you've just had Thanksgiving turkey makes no difference at all. Even if you don't like the royal bird you have it on the table and the same thing goes for cornbread stuffing. There are so many cornbread stuffing recipes that it's always agonizing to choose one, but the one we offer here has been proclaimed "best" by aficionados down South, up North, and out West.

First, a note about roasting the bird. The important thing to remember is that *the new breed of bird cooks faster* and using the usual timing may result in overcooking or drying out an otherwise succulent turkey. Also, those pop-up timers are not entirely reliable. New recommendations: Roast at 325°F. until a minimum temperature of 180°F. registers on a meat thermometer (in the thigh.) Let the bird stand for 20 minutes before carving. It is also recommended that the stuffing be cooked *outside* the bird for unappetizing health reasons.

THE Bordello Cookbook

5 cups cornbread, crumbled into large chunks
6 strips of bacon
1 cup chopped onion
1 cup chopped celery
1 teaspoon dried sage
2 eggs
1 cup buttermilk
1 teaspoon Worcestershire sauce
½ teaspoon Tabasco sauce
Salt and pepper to taste

Place cornbread on a baking sheet and bake in a preheated 300°F. oven until it is dried out; transfer to a large mixing bowl. In a medium skillet, fry bacon until crisp, remove, and crumble, reserving the skillet fat. Sauté onions and celery in the reserved bacon fat until vegetables are softened but not browned.

In a small bowl, whisk together sage, eggs, buttermilk, and seasonings; fold in bacon and sautéed vegetables. Pour over cornbread and toss together until well combined. Bake in a large casserole at 325°F., basting occasionally with turkey pan juices, for 1 hour.

Yield: 2½–3 quarts; enough to serve with Thanksgiving-size turkey

The most exciting Christmas celebration ever staged at Pauline's was centered on a wedding—the marriage of a girl called Terrific to a rich cattleman. Terrific had breached the first law of her profession by falling in love with a customer. Fortunately for her, the customer was equally smitten with Terrific. They both begged Pauline to let them be married at The House on Clay Street, where their romance had blossomed, and further urged her to give the bride away herself.

Pauline protested. "Who ever heard of a wedding in a whorehouse," she said, "Especially on Christmas Day? And who ever heard of a madam giving the bride away? Hell, a madam never gives away anything!"

Nevertheless, the wedding did take place in the parlor house drawing room and Pauline did give the bride away. The bride wore white and Pauline (who was round and plump enough for the role) was dressed in a Santa Claus suit. It's bound to have been the wedding of the decade in Bowling Green, although few of the citizens were favored with an invitation.

The guests were greeted with this lethal potion made with "heavy rum," undoubtedly the Jamaican dark rum popular at the time. In today's punches, Puerto Rican rums or other good island rums are often used.

Wedding Day Punch

Serve cold, cold, cold. And don't visit the punch bowl too often—you'll be sorrrr-eee!

6 lemons, thinly sliced
1 quart brandy
1 pineapple, peeled, cored, and sliced
1 pound sugar
1 quart green tea
1 pint rum
1 quart peach brandy
3 quarts club soda
6 bottles champagne

Place lemons in a large bowl and cover with brandy. Cover and set aside to steep for at least 1 day. Add pineapple to the mixture and let stand for an hour; place mixture in a very large container. Add sugar, tea, rum, and peach brandy, stir well, and refrigerate. To serve, pour mixture over a large block of ice, add club soda, and champagne. Stir to combine.

Yield: 100 servings

THE BORDELLO COOKBOOK

In most Southern clans, the "groom's cake" was a family tradition, often served at the rehearsal supper. This one is unusual in that it combines spice and chocolate cake ingredients to make a delicious dark cake. But it's the moist, fruity topping that makes this dessert a masterpiece.

Groom's Cake Divine

½ cup butter, softened
1 cup sugar
3 eggs, beaten
1 cup buttermilk
2 teaspoons baking soda
3 cups flour
2 tablespoons unsweetened cocoa powder

1 tablespoon ground cinnamon
1 teaspoon ground nutmeg
½ teaspoon ground cloves
½ teaspoon salt
1 apple, peeled and grated

Preheat the oven to 350°F.

In a large bowl, cream butter, and beat in sugar gradually until mixture is light and fluffy. Add eggs, one at a time, beating well after each addition. In a small bowl, sift dry ingredients together. Add alternately to batter with buttermilk. Add grated apple gently to combine. Spoon batter into greased and floured 12 x 9 x 2-inch pan. Bake for 30 minutes, or until golden and cake springs back to the touch. Cool on a wire rack. Remove from pan and top with cooled fruit and nut topping (recipe follows).

Yield: 16 to 18 servings

Fruit Topping for Groom's Cake

3 dried peach halves, chopped
¼ cup peach brandy
1 can (20 ounces) crushed pineapple in its own juice
1 package (7 ounces) shredded coconut
Juice and grated zest of 1 orange
1 cup chopped nuts
½ cup dark brown sugar
½ cup milk

In a medium saucepan, combine chopped dried peaches and peach brandy, and heat over low heat until peaches are plumped, about 5 minutes. Add remaining ingredients to pan and cook over medium heat, stirring constantly, until mixture is thickened, about 10 minutes. Cool. Spread over top of cooled groom's cake.

Since there had been no rehearsal for the free form ceremony, the groom's cake at the wedding on Clay Street was served at the reception that followed—with champagne and a splash of brandy. And whatever happened to the happy couple? When last heard from, their unlikely marriage had lasted twenty-two years, produced four sons, and was still going strong on a prosperous ranch in Texas.

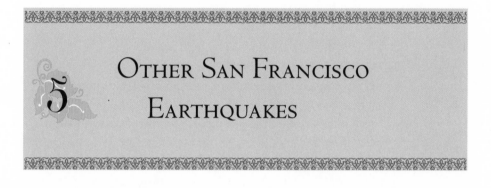

5   OTHER SAN FRANCISCO EARTHQUAKES

The California Gold Rush gave gold digging new dimensions. Estimates had it that San Francisco was headquarters for 10,000 ladies of the blue chamber even before the sidewalks were laid. (No pun intended.) Prospectors often paid up in freshly panned gold, sometimes as much as six ounces per trick. Bella Union, a notorious house operating from 1849 to 1906, featured girls with such promising names as Rotary Rose and Always Ready Rita.

Ready as Rita is, our new pesto pasta dish endows pasta salad with welcome new taste if not total respectability. Contrary to general assumption, pasta salad did not originate in California. It began in Italy as a room-temperature side dish dressed in a medley of tomatoes, basil, olive oil, garlic, and other seasonings. But California did bring it to new heights (or depths as food purists insist). So, yes! Pasta salad, as we know it, is another California innovation. And like energetic Rita, it's always ready because it holds well in the fridge.

Pesto Pasta Salad

In this dish, pasta poses as rice. And, yes, you may indeed substitute rice or another pasta shape if you please.

1 lb. orzo (rice-shaped pasta) cooked al dente, rinsed, and
    drained
2 cups basil leaves (or 1 cup *each* of basil and parsley)
4 cloves garlic
½ cup blanched almonds (or walnuts)
Salt and pepper to taste
½ cup olive oil
½ cup grated Parmesan cheese

Place cooked orzo in a large serving bowl. Combine remaining ingredients in a food processor and process until well blended. Add the pesto sauce to the pasta and toss to combine. Serve cold or at room temperature as a salad, side dish, or appetizer. (To make a hearty main dish, add meat, fish, or poultry.)

Yield: 6 to 8 servings

Note: Originally, pesto sauce was made by using a mortar and pestle. We prefer the food processor, but like the pesto to have some texture instead of blending until it's perfectly smooth.

Perhaps the most discussed madam in the early history of San Francisco was a Baltimore minister's daughter, Belle Cora, whose previous base was New Orleans. She had fled the piety of the parsonage in her early teens to become one of the most versatile bawds in the business. The range of her offerings may be suggested by a vintage photograph of her in a West Coast picture gallery, which showed her posed bestride a toy horse with a clutch of whips at the ready.

One of the most popular attractions in San Francisco was Madam Gareilles's "Virgin Room," wherein gullible customers were introduced to a professional virgin who performed a scripted routine with unsuspecting and misinformed johns. For a hefty price, the routine could be spied on through peepholes by other customers, some of whom had been taken in by the virgin story earlier—and had been watched through the same peepholes. The humiliation of the new victim was balm to the men who had endured the deception before and they eagerly helped the house recruit new customers to "deflower" the veteran actress.

At the "better parlor houses" the madams tried to compensate for such flagrant behavior by prettying up the premises and serving food and drinks that suggested a modicum of refinement. One was a "nightcap" called a Brandy Pillow, which at the time was a simple mix of brandy, milk, and sugar—and if there was no brandy in the house, they cheerfully substituted anything alcoholic that was on hand. Here's one worthy of your finest cognac:

Brandy Pillow

½ pint sherbet
½ pint vanilla ice cream
½ cup brandy
Ice cubes

Place all ingredients except ice cubes in blender and whirl until combined. Add ice cubes, one at a time, and whirl until the mixture is the consistency of soft ice cream. Pour into stemmed sherbet glasses.

Yield: 4 servings

Note: If you have silver serving cups/glasses and not many excuses to use them, you may want to frost them and serve your Brandy Pillows in those.

Frittata

The clever madams also put together easy egg dishes to serve overnight guests or hungry customers at any time of the day or night. Some of them were similar to the *frittatas* of today. The *frittata* is an Italian omelet. Unlike the French omelet that is folded, the *frittata* has the ingredients mixed throughout the eggs. The variations, as you might imagine, are endless. A few favorites are included here.

2 tablespoons olive oil, divided
2 cloves garlic, minced
1 onion, thinly sliced
4 cups thinly sliced peppers (a tricolor combination of red, yellow, and green peppers)
½ teaspoon salt
½ teaspoon pepper
8 eggs
½ cup grated Parmesan cheese

Preheat the oven to 325°F. In a large skillet, heat 1 tablespoon olive oil, and add garlic and onions. Sauté over medium heat until onion is wilted. Add peppers, salt, and pepper and simmer until peppers are soft. Set aside.

In a large bowl, beat eggs lightly, and add pepper mixture. Heat remaining tablespoon of olive oil in a large oven-proof skillet and pour in egg mixture; sprinkle top with grated cheese. Reduce heat and cook until sides begin to set. Transfer skillet to preheated oven and bake for 15 to 20 minutes, until *frittata* is golden. Serve immediately, cut into wedges.

Yield: 8 servings

Note: Fans of leftover frittata claim that it's even better served cold or at room temperature, and some even make a sandwich of it. Our read on this is that the best frittata is the one you like best. (Just like the famous adage about wine.)

SOME FRITTATA VARIATIONS

Spinach: Substitute 2 cups cooked, drained spinach for the peppers and add ¼ teaspoon ground nutmeg.

Potato: Substitute 2 cups sliced, cooked potatoes for the peppers and add ½ cup shredded Swiss cheese in place of the Parmesan.

Tomato–Zucchini: Substitute 1 cup each chopped tomatoes and zucchini for the peppers and add ¼ cup chopped fresh basil.

By 1853, San Francisco had forty-eight first-class parlor houses, 150

THE Bordello Cookbook

second-class establishments, plus numberless dens and cribs. And, as in biblical times, tents were set up for girls in some areas beside makeshift bars. The bars were nothing more than broad planks supported by barrels but steady enough to hold a few jugs of the going rot gut.

Lola Montez, famed as the mistress of King Louis I of Bavaria, arrived not only to ply her sexual talents among the nouveau riche panners and plunderers but to win stardom on the stage, lecturing and dancing her highly original version of the jig. Lola's box-office appeal was jet-propelled by the rumor that she had once given King Louis ten orgasms in twenty-four hours, a feat which more than one customer challenged her to match—with him! The scandal caused by her antics with the king had brought about his abdication, which proved to be just one more credential in the resumé of a grand courtesan. *Whatever Lola Wants, Lola Gets* could have been her theme song, her previous trophies having included Alexander Dumas, and Père and Franz Liszt. But her fling with the king was her finest hour. She now rests from her exertions in a Brooklyn cemetery.

Dolly Adams, hailed as the girl in the fishbowl, made her debut onstage at the Bella Union Theater, circa 1873, billed as "The Water Queen." Her act was an exhibition of diving, swimming, and other unspectacular maneuvers performed in a glass tank of water that was wheeled up to the footlights by gawking stage hands. Dolly was only eleven years old but she was both endowed and experienced enough to pass for seventeen. Since her water exercises were unremarkable at best, her paid audience was compensated mainly by her bathing suit, which, for the times, was eye-poppingly scant and tight.

As San Francisco prospered, "society" began to take shape and the nouveau riche vulgarians who dominated it undoubtedly deserved the ridicule they inspired in song and doggerel. Perhaps the most memorable of the latter was the oft-quoted quatrain by one anonymous rhymester:

> The miners came in forty-nine
> The whores in fifty-one
> And when they got together
> They produced the native son.

Some of the shady ladies did, indeed, marry men of wealth and status. One, who had been christened Caroline Decker Smith, operated a series of sex parlors under the names Maud Thomas, Maud Corrigan, Maud Ulman and, finally, Maud Nelson. She retired to become Maud Nelson Fair, daughter-in-law of James G. Fair, the Comstock Lode millionaire and former United States senator. Her husband was the ex-Senator's second son, Charley, a devout alcoholic and all-round debauchee. The *Oakland Tribune* gleefully reported that Charles L. Fair had married "a tall and exceedingly stout blonde," adding that "Fair was perfectly steady and did not appear to have been drinking."

Champagne was far and away the elixir of choice at the parlor houses, often generating more profit to the madams than the tricks. The houses became such important outlets for the wine merchants that several of them were said to be major underwriters of the establishments, providing the madams everything from rent to bail money—and, as a special token of their appreciation, free bubbly for their semi-annual celebrations of *joie de vivre*.

A favorite dish at these celebrations was salmon poached in champagne and this updated recipe wins special praise. It makes a particularly impressive appearance on a buffet served in an interesting fish dish, or on a salmon board, with sprigs of dill for garnish.

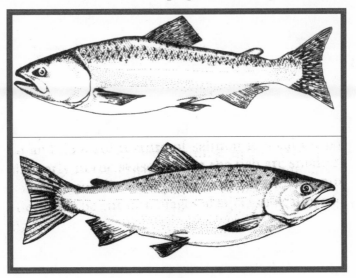

Salmon Poached in Champagne

A 5- to 6-pound whole salmon, cleaned and boned
1 orange, thinly sliced
1 large onion, thinly sliced

CALIFORNIA CUCUMBER SAUCE

A good accompaniment to salmon poached in champagne is this refreshing sauce:

1 large cucumber, peeled and seeded
1 cup water
1 tablespoon salt
¼ cup sugar
¼ cup white vinegar
1 cup sour cream
Paprika, for garnish, optional

Thinly slice cucumber and place in a bowl with the water, salt, sugar, and vinegar. Stir to combine. Cover and set aside for 1 hour or longer. Drain cucumber and fold into sour cream. Dust with paprika, if desired.

Yield: 2½ cups

2 lemons, thinly sliced
3 strips of bacon
1 split California champagne
Fresh dill sprigs, for garnish

Preheat the oven to 400°F. Lay salmon on its side on a large piece of heavy foil. Fill salmon cavity with slices of orange, onion, and 1 of the lemons. Arrange remaining lemon slices on the salmon and top with bacon strips. Transfer to a large roasting pan, turning up edges of the foil to form a dish. Pour champagne over all. Cover with another piece of heavy-duty foil, folding edges to seal. Place in preheated oven for 35 to 45 minutes, or until fish flakes easily with a fork. Serve immediately. Or, if this is to be a buffet dish, let cool and chill.

Yield: 8 to 10 servings

Edward M. Greenway, an ambitious salesman who had struck it rich as the exclusive agent for an acclaimed brand of champagne, was the social arbiter of early San Francisco. The wealth he acquired from champagne sales commissions bought enough influence for him to found a loosely structured organization known as the Bachelors' Cotillion Club. Through the club he quickly became the debutante dictator, launching the coveted "Greenway dances"—a series of elegant winter social events whose invitation lists were prepared by him alone. His choices were based not only on the attributes of the girls and the affluence of their families but on his personal rapport with their family members. A commentator of the era explained that regardless of a deb's beauty or prominent family connections, she could be passed up because Greenway harbored an "old grudge against her father or because her mother's gold teeth gave him the jitters." Whatever the

THE BORDELLO COOKBOOK

reason, a deb who failed to make the invitation list was a social failure—period—and spent the winter scheming ways to amend the disaster.

Meanwhile, on the other side of town, the busiest operator in the sex trade was an import from China named Ah Toy who, for a time, was the only Chinese whore in San Francisco. Since only the oldest, ugliest bawds in the business (black or white) would accommodate Chinese men, the sons of China formed lines that wrapped around the block, waiting as long as six hours for a four minute fling with Ah

Toy. Chinese men were pouring into San Francisco by the boatload to build the roads and bridges and houses and the only women available to them were the dregs of the business. Rather than settle for a toothless old hag, they'd wait all day for a turn with one of their own young beauties.

After months of overwork, Ah Toy at last acquired help. Another Chinese girl hit town eager to make easy money and immediately set up shop with the exhausted Toy. As the Chinese immigration continued, the pair recruited other newly arrived golden girls and soon Ah Toy was running a series of extremely busy bagnios. In spite of her early exertion, Ah Toy lived to be one hundred years old and died rich, never once having regretted that the San Francisco of her youth was so politically incorrect.

Politically correct or not, San Francisco's Chinatown today creates some of the best cuisine on the planet and the hot chicken salad that originated there is one of the city's social darlings.

Chicken Salad (Warm)

One 2½- to 3-pound chicken, cleaned and trussed
1 head iceberg lettuce, shredded
1 bunch scallions, including tops, thinly sliced
1 bunch cilantro, chopped
¼ cup sesame seeds, toasted
3 ounces translucent Chinese noodles, fried according to
    package directions
Lemon Soy Sauce (recipe follows)

Preheat oven to 400°F.

Roast chicken for about 1 hour, or until juices run clear;
Let stand for 5 to 10 minutes at room temperature. Remove
crispy skin and meat from chicken and chop. Place in a
large salad bowl and add remaining ingredients, tossing well
with lemon soy sauce. Serve at once while chicken is still
warm.

Yield: 4 servings

LEMON SOY SAUCE

¾ cup salad oil
1 tablespoon lemon juice
1 tablespoon soy sauce
1 teaspoon sugar
1 teaspoon grated lemon peel
1 teaspoon prepared mustard
1 clove garlic, minced

Combine ingredients in a bowl
and whisk until blended.

Yield: 1 cup sauce

Note: There is a solid group of Californians that prefers to wrap the chicken salad in iceberg lettuce leaves instead of adding shredded lettuce to the mixture. Another group, just as solid, adds the shredded lettuce and wraps the portions in lettuce leaves as well. How you serve it is up to you (and how much you like iceberg lettuce).

THE BORDELLO COOKBOOK

Chinese Almond Cookies

The favored dessert to follow warm Chicken Salad is (what else?) Chinese Almond Cookies and none we have ever bought in a store can even approach these.

¾ cup vegetable shortening
¾ cup sugar
2 eggs
1 tablespoon almond extract
3 cups flour
1 teaspoon baking soda
¼ teaspoon salt
1 cup blanched almond halves

Preheat oven to 350°F.

In the large bowl of an electric mixer, beat shortening until light and fluffy. Add the sugar gradually, continuing to beat until the mixture is smooth. Beat in 1 of the eggs and the almond extract.

Meanwhile, sift together the flour, baking soda, and salt. Slowly add dry ingredients to the shortening mixture. The dough will be very stiff.

Using a teaspoon, scoop small pieces of the dough and, using your hands, roll into 1-inch balls. Place balls 2 inches apart on lightly greased cookie sheets. Flatten each ball with your hand or the bottom of a glass to a thickness of ½ inch; press an almond half (split side down) into the top of each cookie. Lightly beat the remaining egg and brush the tops of the cookies with egg.

Bake in the preheated oven for 15 minutes, or until golden. Remove while hot to a cooling rack. Cool completely and store in an airtight container.

Yield: 4 dozen cookies

Note: For "good luck," you may want to brush the almonds with red food coloring before you brush each cookie with beaten egg. (Red means "good luck" in Chinese.)

Of all the whores in all the towns all over the world, one goes down in history and up in humankind as the absolute mama of them all. She was Sally Stanford, described by the press after her retirement as "San Francisco's madam emeritus" and before as "San Francisco's number-one business woman." The latter description was not overflow from the journalistic hyperbole that ran rampant at the time. It was on target. Sally was brilliant, inventive, and super-savvy—as well as sly, lawless, and super-tough! Her continuing battles with the police landed her in court many times where she picked up a store of legal expertise that confounded adversaries on both sides of the law. Eventually, the newspapers were to gasp out the news that the veteran sex merchant had become Madam Mayor, the duly elected chief executive of Sausalito, California, key city of fashionable Marin County.

During her colorful career in vice, Sally operated under twenty-eight different names, several of them legal. Among the latter was Mrs. Robert Livingston Gump, the name she acquired when she married a scion of the multimillionaire family whose fortune derived from their dealership in Oriental *objets d'art*.

Stanford, however, was the name that Sally liked best and kept longest—in fact, until she died. She took it as her own on a Saturday afternoon when she had bet heavily on a football game between Stanford University and the University of California. Stanford won the game, Sally won her bet, and the university won an unlikely new namesake. From time to time, Sally owned and operated an uncounted number of illicit houses. Chief among them was "The Fortress," which columnist Herb Caen habitually referred to as "The Sally Stanford School of Advanced Social Studies." Caen's wit was no doubt inspired by the madam's habit of referring to her hostesses in residence as "my debutantes."

Never mind the names. Sally Stanford was simply The Ultimate Madam and "The Fortress" was The Ultimate Whorehouse. The imposing mansion at 1144 Pine Street, where the social studies were conducted, had been built by Robert G. Hanford for his mistress, chocolate heiress Gabrielle Guittard, who after several scandal-riddled years final-

ly became his third wife. The formidable stone structure was all but impenetrable, guarded by heavy iron gates and a battery of automatically locking doors that were manned by stalwart gatekeepers and doormen. The major attraction inside was a drop-dead Pompeian court, 50 by 138 feet. On a dais at one end of the fountain-centered court was a much-publicized marble bathtub, an enduring curio that had once been owned by Anna Held, a star in the firmament of Flo Ziegfeld. With a typical Ziegfeld touch, the impresario had announced that Anna was addicted to leisurely milk baths and had purchased the marble tub as the proper vessel for these luxurious rites.

This undoubtedly did wonders for the milk industry, which currently spends millions a year promoting the efficacy of its product to a world that is increasingly preoccupied with "fat free" and "low cholesterol" invaders. At any rate, in the good old days of Anna Held and Flo

Ziegfeld there was a rage for desserts that made the most of rich creams, whipped cream, and ice cream. A specialty was Bombe Glacé, a most spectacular creation. It was made in a spherical mold—the mold coated inside with good store-bought ice cream and the center filled with luscious, often exotic, mixtures. The filling can be varied to suit your mood and menu and although the recipe sounds complex, it's really quite easy, requiring mainly patience.

Bombe Extraordinaire

(for a 2½-quart mold)
3 pints rich vanilla ice cream
2 pints raspberry sherbet (or sorbet)
½ cup Chambord liqueur
6 chocolate-covered toffee candy bars, broken into bite-sized pieces
1 cup heavy cream
1 tablespoon powdered sugar
Fresh raspberries, for garnish
½ cup toasted almonds, for garnish

Soften ice cream in refrigerator until spreadable, then spread it evenly to line the mold. Cover and freeze until ice cream is firm, about half an hour. Meanwhile soften raspberry sherbet the same way and stir Chambord into the sherbet to blend. Spread the sherbet mixture evenly over the vanilla ice cream, leaving a well in the center of the mold; cover and freeze until firm. Fill the well with candy pieces; cover and freeze again until firm. About 1 hour before serving, invert mold on top of a chilled serving platter; freeze.

Whip cream until soft peaks form, add powdered sugar, and continue beating

---

SOME BOMBE VARIATIONS

Choco-Mint: Coat mold with rich chocolate ice cream, spread with mint ice cream laced with *crème de menthe*, and fill the well with buttered toasted walnut pieces.

Brandied Peach: Coat mold with peach ice cream, spread with lemon sherbet and fill the well with sliced, fresh peaches macerated in brandy.

Tropical Island: Coat mold with rich lemon custard ice cream, spread with mango sherbet, and fill the well with shredded coconut sprinkled with rum.

The Bordello Cookbook

until peaks form again. Spoon whipped cream into a pastry bag and decorate bombe. Freeze.

To serve, garnish bombe with fresh raspberries and toasted slivered almonds. Let stand a few minutes for easier slicing. Cut bombe into wedges, spooning candy bits over each wedge.

Yield: 12 servings

Sally prospered prodigiously at The Fortress, but her happiness was marred by one Sgt. John Dyer of the San Francisco Police Department Vice Squad. Dyer devoted his career to an Odyssean effort to "nail" her on charges of prostitution. Sally was quoted as saying that "What Ahab was to Moby Dick, tracking that whale down for years, had nothing on Dyer trying to track me down." Although he is reputed to have wrecked his health trying to invade The Fortress, Sally always outsmarted him. He was successful in getting her arrested only once and that was after she had vacated The Fortress to take up lesser quarters during World War II. (Patriotism, you know!)

Tiring of her continuing harassment by the San Francisco police, Sally moved across the Golden Gate Bridge to picturesque Sausalito, where she opened a gourmet restaurant that was in the vanguard of California's epidemic nouvelle cuisine. She called the restaurant Valhalla and decorated it in a style reminiscent of her old profession. One patron of the place recalls that the tables were centered by chamber pots holding bouquets of fresh flowers.

Sally was a capital cook whose taste and artistry in the kitchen launched dozens of inventive new dishes that sparked the trend to light eating. Living as she did in the San Francisco area she had access to the bounty of fresh fruits and vegetables cultivated in California's famous growing centers—to say nothing of the fine local wines that were starting to rival (and even best) some of the vintage products of France and Italy.

One of Sally's most popular dishes was *cioppino*, which is the Bay Area's rendition of a good fish chowder. It is probably more similar to Manhattan chowders because it is tomato based rather than dairy based as New England chowder is. The choice of fish to be used in the recipe below depends on availability and your personal preferences. There is loud argument as to whether the wine for *cioppino* should be red or white, but we vote for red every time, both *in* and *with*.

Cioppino

3 pounds firm-fleshed fish
1 pound large shrimp, peeled and deveined
1 pint clams, mussels, or oysters (or a combination of all 3)
1 Dungeness crab or medium lobster, cooked and chopped
¾ cup olive oil
1 cup chopped onion
1 cup chopped green pepper
1 clove garlic, minced
1 large can (2½ pounds) chopped tomatoes
1 large can (46 ounces) tomato juice
2 cups dry red wine
1 bay leaf
1 tablespoon fresh chopped basil
Salt and pepper to taste
½ cup minced fresh parsley

Cut fish into serving-size pieces. Use heads plus crab or lobster shells to make a fish stock to be added later. Steam clams, mussels, and/or oysters using just a small amount of water. Reserve broth to add later.

In a large saucepan, heat olive oil, add onion, green pepper, and garlic, and sauté until soft. Add tomatoes, tomato juice, wine, basil, and salt and pepper, plus 2 cups of the fish stock and shellfish broth. Cook for about 15 minutes.

Layer fish and shrimp in a large serving kettle. Add the tomato mixture. Cover and simmer for about 15 minutes. Add the Dungeness crab or lobster, cover, and simmer for 5 minutes. Add clams, mussels, and/or oysters, cover, and simmer for 2 minutes, or until the fish flakes easily, the shrimp is done, and the shellfish heated through. Correct the seasonings and serve immediately, garnished with chopped parsley.

Yield: 10 to 12 servings

Note: Crusty bread and hearty red wine are all you need to complete this meal.

Lentil Salad

Another Stanford standby was lentil salad, long enjoyed in the West as an hors d'oeuvre, salad, or side dish and especially popular with vegetarians. Lentil salad was originally of French derivation but this recipe has been given a Middle Eastern twist with the addition of cumin, tumeric, coriander, and yogurt.

2 cups lentils, rinsed
1 bay leaf
½ cup chopped red onion
½ cup chopped carrot
1 clove garlic, minced
¼ cup olive oil
1 tablespoon lemon juice
1 teaspoon ground cumin
½ teaspoon ground tumeric
½ teaspoon ground coriander
Salt and pepper to taste
½ cup plain yogurt
¼ cup chopped fresh parsley

In a medium saucepan, cover lentils with cold water and add bay leaf. Bring water to a boil and simmer for about 10 minutes. Add chopped onion and carrot and cook until tender. Drain and cool. Add garlic, lemon juice, oil, and seasonings. Mix lightly. Cover and refrigerate for an hour or overnight. To serve, top each portion with a dollop of yogurt and sprinkle with parsley.

Yield: 6 servings

Angel's Kiss Cocktail

The bar in Sally's Valhalla was much admired not only for the dazzling wine list but for creative libations like the romantic Angel's Kiss, a frothy after-dinner drink:

¼ ounce *crème de cacao* (chocolate liqueur)
¼ ounce *crème de yvette* (violet liqueur)
¼ ounce brandy
¼ ounce light cream
Crushed ice
Maraschino cherry, for garnish

Shake first 5 ingredients together. Strain into a stemmed glass and top with a cherry.

Yield: 1 cocktail

Long accustomed to battling the authorities, Sally's displeasure with what she considered the stupidity of Sausalito's civic leaders lead her to take on the city council. With relish! Her aim in life now was to "Keep Sausalito Sausalito," by blocking the invasion of industry that threatened to spoil the rustic charm of this picture-postcard community. To put her ideas into action, she ran for a seat on the City Council and, using the hammer-and-tongs tactics on her Sausalito opponents that she had lavished on the San Francisco police, won election. She was so effective on the council that her neighbors decided she was right and elected her Mayor of Sausalito. In spite of her flaming past, Sally was much admired across the country as an exemplary mayor, and many of her programs for the city were widely copied. But with typical individuality, Sally Stanford always said that "the best part of being Mayor is the fun of being called Madam Mayor."

THE BIG BUZZ IN L.A.: QUEEN BEE

She was a celebrity in Celebrity Land, owner and operator of a long, glittering string of bordellos in the big-money areas of Los Angeles. Because her clientele was heavily weighted toward the high-profile film colonists she was known as "Madam of the Stars." It was a title that clearly pleased her but she always responded with unfelt modesty that she was a "simple nookie bookie."

Simple she never was. Beverly Davis was a psychiatric study who could have baffled the whole shrinking profession. Apparently, most of the women in the U.S.A. who have engaged in prostitution turned to it as a possible escape from poverty. But Beverly had other motivations. She came from a well-to-do family with no particular financial worries, but they had a casebook full of emotional problems that money couldn't help.

Beverly was French—at the top of her voice. She had been born in America but at an early age adopted her mother's birthplace, which was Paris. She delighted in salting her conversation with little French phrases that she considered chic and referred to her adored mother always as *Maman*. As for her father, who was also French but internationally disagreeable and confused, she called him several unadoring things, in plain-to-raw English. The main trouble was that Daddy Dearest (one Gaston Dubois) suspected *Maman* of continuing

infidelity and was convinced that Beverly—their fifth child—was not of his doing. This daughter, declared he, was the out-of-bounds offspring of an old flame with whom *Maman* had carried on before she married him—and who had a way of showing up again from time to time.

Whether Gaston's suspicions were valid or not, the name of this old flame was (guess what?)—Beverly!—and, though Daddy Dearest knew it, *Maman* cavalierly chose it as the name for her new daughter.

"It wasn't true," Beverly insisted, years later. "I wish to God it was but the fact is that I am my father's own child. No doubt about it. I got his terrible temper and a couple of other nasty traits he had that make me hate myself sometimes, almost as much as I hated him. I was like a boy—independent as a *gamin*, he used to say—which was, politely, street urchin. He didn't like that and he didn't like me and I didn't like him. So at least we agreed on something!"

At any rate, he could hardly wait until she was old enough to be shipped off to a convent for schooling by the nuns, which happened the day she was six.

Beverly despised the convent and the nuns. She denounced the

THE BORDELLO COOKBOOK

sisters as a pack of gypsies and rewarded their efforts in her behalf by cursing them roundly in French. They were determined to transform the hot-tempered child into a sweet and demure little lady but had they succeeded even dimly it would have been a miracle straight out of the New Testament. The fact was that Beverly also despised being a girl and eventually would run the sexual gamut, first as a lesbian, then bisexual and prostitute, up for anything—the kinkier, the better! Meanwhile she did everything she could think of to make everybody else as miserable as she was. She missed her *Maman* but, instead of crying, she fought. She'd pick a fight with anybody right up to the Sister Superior and when she was punished she merely attacked again with renewed fury. Woe to her disciplinarian!

Beverly especially detested the convent's plain, tasteless food ("Everything's gray!" she protested. "It even *tastes* gray!") and after the exotic French fare served by *Maman*, she found it revolting. Her favorite flavor was lemon and *Maman* had a big repertoire of lemon desserts to delight Beverly and irritate Gaston—who was "a devout chocolate man." (The nuns' idea of dessert, Beverly said, was a raw apple.)

Lemon Pudding Cake (Lemon Lust)

Our own lemon pudding cake would have made the cut at Chez Dubois because it never fails to captivate anybody who likes lemon—and who, besides Gaston, doesn't? The cooking method gives you a delicious twosome—pudding on the bottom, sponge cake on the top. What's more it's simple, easy, inexpensive and so good that it has been called Lemon Lust. This is one you'll be serving again and again as a welcome finale for family or company dinners.

3 eggs, separated
1 cup sugar
1 cup milk
2 tablespoons flour
2 lemons

Preheat the oven to 350°F.

In the small mixer bowl, beat egg yolks until combined; add

sugar gradually, beating until mixture thickens and sugar is dissolved. Add milk and flour, beating to combine. Remove zest from lemons, grate, and add to batter along with juice from lemons. In a small bowl, beat egg whites until stiff; fold into batter. Pour batter into a 1½-quart soufflé dish or casserole. Place dish in a pan of hot water so that the water comes at least halfway up the side of the baking dish. Bake in preheated oven for about 1 hour. Remove from oven, lift out of the water bath, and cool on a rack at room temperature. Serve with whipped cream, if desired.

Yield: 6 servings

On orders from her father the nuns intercepted and destroyed letters to Beverly written by *Maman* as well as those that Beverly wrote to her mother, so that for eight years she felt totally abandoned. At age fourteen she ran away, simply slipping out of the convent one afternoon with nothing but the clothes on her back. On the train to San Francisco without a ticket or money, she was befriended by an understanding madam, and thus began one of the most colorful vice careers in the history of California.

Beverly prospered as a prostitute working for the friendly madam and at age sixteen had squirreled away enough money to open a house of her own. Always ambitious, she wanted a first-class place and got auxiliary funding from a wine salesman. As noted elsewhere in these pages, champagne was the drink of choice in the bagnios and the wine merchants were always eager to help a new madam get a start. With his assistance, she leased the entire top floor of an apartment hotel at the corner of Davis and Sloane streets in San Francisco. The hotel fronted on Davis and the location proved so successful that Beverly took the name as her own. "Goodbye forever to Beverly Dubois. Say hello, world, to Beverly Davis!" Friends and newspaper columnists would later shorten her first name to Bee but, in honor of *Maman*'s old flame, she continued to sign it as Beverly all her life.

The new madam was a great natural. Her premises had eighteen suites with private baths and four parlors. Instinctively she knew that it

would be bad business to compete with the girls who worked for her—and she didn't. She got half of the money they made anyway, so why be greedy? Why not just have a glass of wine with the fellows and turn them over to her girls? "This wasn't always easy," she said. "Because a lot of guys insist on having the madam. They assume that if she's in charge she must be gooooood!"

Occasionally, she did take on an insistent client but usually her energies were expended on planning and hostessing dinner parties, after which she turned the johns over to her girls. They appreciated her ethics and she had no problem recruiting and keeping "top-quality girls."

Meanwhile, the sunshine of Southern California, together with the burgeoning movie industry, was growing new opportunities for sex vendeuses and, Beverly, cash rich now and richly experienced, moved on to Los Angeles. "San Francisco is getting over-whored anyway," she complained.

Her first place in L.A. was in Belmore, "the heart of the millionaire mansion district." Beverly wanted only the clientele with deep pockets and to attract them did everything possible to assure them privacy and discretion. Her number was unlisted and she would never say anything to anyone on the phone until she was absolutely sure who

was on the line. Neither would she allow clients to be called to the telephone. Further, the johns were asked not to arrive in taxis because streams of cabs bringing men to the house would attract attention. Her place, which was discreetly set back from the street, was operated as a private club and customers came there in their own cars or in Delman limousines. Delman's, of course, got a rake-off.

Beverly much preferred the limo traffic and encouraged the men to use Delman's because the private cars gave her a problem. Girls were not supposed to "date clients on the side," and they could get the real names and addresses of their johns by taking their license plate numbers and checking with friends in the police bureau. When this happened, it was an obvious risk for everybody and Beverly immediately fired the offending girl.

Dinner at the Belmore house was always an extravaganza and though no menus survive we know that any soiree there was sophisticated and lavish. Calories and cholesterol had not yet become a national preoccupation and clients ate with more enthusiasm than restraint. Dinner, typically, was a dazzling parade of foods such as these:

Cocktails: Cheese balls with macadamia nuts, steak tartare, caviar, lobster croquettes, and many exotic aspics—plus all the martinis and Manhattans you could imagine.

First course: Asparagus soup (creamed, of course)

The Bordello Cookbook

accompanied by cheese straws.

Entrée: Planked steak—whole loin of beef wrapped in bacon and served with brandied mushrooms.

Side dishes: A variety of vegetables—stuffed, scalloped, or sautéed, many prepared *au gratin* (with bread crumbs, butter and/or cheese).

Salads: Endlessly fussed over with mayonnaise and French dressing predominating. Also elaborate molded salads, ultra-rich and creamy. California, which we think of as the salad bowl of America, served up few of the light, low-calorie kind that we insist on today.

Desserts: Dramatic and glamorous, often flamed or flambéed. Many of these grand finales reflected the ethnic heritage of the Hollywood moguls, with European cakes and cookies included.

It should be observed that dinner in Los Angeles now at the fashionable restaurants and bistros is definitely something else. It is presided over not by an eager-to-please madam, but a health guru. Both lunch and dinner are disdained as nothing if a couple of these are not included:

Bottled waters: From far-flung places (the farther flung the better).

Consommé: Vegetable, preferably, meatless.

Macrobiotic salad: strange, unidentified flora, some of which look downright poisonous.

Fresh fruits: The most esoteric and expensive that grow.

Enough of today's fixations! Back to the indulgences of yesterday. Beverly's Belmore house had something for everyone and freedom reigned. The place was also popular with women but they were welcome only in the afternoons. They were charged more, too, because the madam said they took up more of the girls' time. For women who preferred men (and for men partial to their own sex), the house maintained a "call file" with the phone numbers, descriptions, and "specialties" of a variety of males—mostly unemployed actors who are always plentiful in Hollywood.

The elaborate dining facilities in the Belmore location were popular, Beverly said, with "all sexes." Culinary ideas from south of the border have always influenced California cuisine and a favorite dish there was picadillo, a hash-like Mexican mixture used for filling tamales, tacos, and meat pies. Creative Californians keep the mixture at the ready for all kinds of socializing. At cocktails they scoop it up with taco chips, but they enjoy it at dinner, too, as either a first course or the main event. (See note below). Here is our own switch on the Belmore chef's recipe.

Picadillo

1 pound ground beef
1 pound ground pork
1 cup chopped onion
2 cloves garlic, minced
1 can (16 ounces), tomatoes, including juice
1 tablespoon vinegar
1 teaspoon ground cinnamon
½ teaspoon ground cumin
½ teaspoon dried oregano
1 bay leaf
1 can (6 ounces) tomato paste
1 can (6 ounces) pitted black olives, chopped
1 cup slivered almonds
1 cup raisins
Salt and pepper to taste

In a large skillet, brown meats together over medium heat. Skim fat, and add onions, garlic, tomatoes, vinegar, cinnamon, cumin, oregano, and bay leaf, stirring to combine. Add tomato paste and 2 cups water. Cover and simmer for 1 hour. Add remaining ingredients and simmer for another 30 minutes.

Yield: 8 entrée servings; 12 to 15 servings as an appetizer or first course

Note: For a first course, serve picadillo over a square of sautéed polenta. As a main course, serve as a taco/tostado or as filling for pita bread or a roll. You might also enjoy it the Cuban way, with rice and black beans.

Beverly described the Belmore House as a gold mine and her sex business in L.A. ballooned into an industry. After the Belmore coup, she operated houses on Sedgmont Street, DeLambert Avenue, North Fairmont, Redfern Drive, Frankfort Avenue, North Delaware, Princess Road, and La Reina Drive in the fashionable hills of Santa Monica. They were all big money makers, all lovingly looked after by the meticulous madam.

She was especially fond of the Princess Road place because "it was so gorgeously furnished and had so many subtle little features that caught the lookers unaware—what you might call suggestive decorations. It was so much fun that married men of affairs trickled in with their wives to show 'em a real Davis sporting house." She didn't

say what the decorations were, but there's no doubt what they suggested.

The place on North Fairmont was called the House of All Nations because the girls employed there were an exotic mix of colors and races. There were Chinese, Japanese, and Spanish girls, one who said she was from Martinque and others who were quadroons and octoroons from the islands and the U.S.A. The house was wildly popular, but it gave Beverly her worst personnel headaches.

"The yellow girls had their own dining room and parlors and lived separately from the whites," she said. "The whites hated them because the yellow girls made more money than they did. As for the blacks of every shade, they were the busiest of all. The white girls were always sore at them because they didn't understand why they got so many customers. I have my own theory about that. Most of our customers were white and I think white men don't want to get in bed with any woman who might remind them of somebody in their own family or social circle. A colored woman of any shade—yellow, black, tan, beige or whatever—isn't going to give them the heebee-jeebies, like maybe they're bedding somebody they shouldn't."

Whatever the reason, the House of All Nations was so successful that Beverly staffed the Princess Road place the same way and called it International House. "That was smart if I do say so myself," she said. "Clientele from half the studios in Hollywood went through it night after night."

The chef at the House of All Nations knew a great deal about California fruits and vegetables because he was an immigrant who, as a teenager, had been a "picker," following the crops to harvest whatever was ripe for picking. He was a significant factor in popularizing guacamole, which he particularly liked himself and enjoyed serving to the johns with cocktails. He explained that California produces the very best avocado for guacamole—the Haas variety, which many picky customers pass up because they are put off by the pebbly, black skin. "Don't be!" he cautioned. "This avocado is superior in every way!"— and we heartily endorse his pronouncement.

THE BORDELLO COOKBOOK

House of All Nations Guacamole

4 ripe Haas avocados, peeled and pitted
Juice of 1 lemon
½ cup diced fresh tomato
¼ cup chopped cilantro
¼ cup minced scallions
2 fresh serrano chilies, seeded and minced
Salt to taste

In a medium bowl, mash avocados with a fork, and add remaining ingredients, stirring to combine. Serve with taco chips.

Yield: 3 cups

Note: You may substitute ½ cup drained hot salsa for the tomato/cilantro/scallion/chili combination—a very quick fix!

Still to come was Beverly's crowning achievement, her North Estabrook "resort." This was a Moorish-style white stucco triplex with a red-tile roof covering forty-six rooms. The camouflage for the operation was an elegant French restaurant, which occupied the first floor and, since the madam was known to many friends and customers as Bee, it was called (with wicked humor) The Beehive. On the lawn, The Beehive's huge neon sign was adorned with a black and gold queen bee that traveled around the sign buzzing out a welcome. On the second floor were the bedroom suites. They were wired to the restaurant and a platoon of waiters rushed trays all day and most of the night to the johns and their girls "upstairs." On the third floor were reception rooms and two bars where customers were greeted by the girls and, often, by the Queen Bee herself. There was also a private dining room on the third floor for very special occasions—and at The Beehive there were lots that were very special, indeed. The third floor chef was hailed as a genius. Beverly doted on him because, like *Maman*, he had been born in France, but he had lived in California long enough to lighten up on his sauces and create a succession of exotic but delicate dishes. "He's a temperamental bastard," Beverly complained, "but there's not a better cook on the West Coast."

Shrimp Pacifica

Since Southern California is both a citrus capital and the mother lode of vegetables and seafood, the third floor chef had access to the gamut of ingredients used in the food that swept the country as nouvelle cuisine. One of his prize inventions was a shrimp and orange first course that became as famous as he was and from this we have derived Shrimp Pacifica. We like it enough to mound it on salad greens and make a meal of it.

6 large navel oranges, peeled, sliced, and quartered

5 red onions, thinly sliced

2 pounds shrimp, deveined, and cooked

1½ cups cider vinegar

1 cup light olive oil

⅔ cup lemon juice

½ cup ketchup

¼ cup minced fresh parsley

1 tablespoon prepared mustard

1 tablespoon sugar

1 teaspoon celery seed

½ teaspoon dried red pepper flakes

2 cloves garlic, minced

Salt and pepper to taste

Place oranges, onions, and shrimp in a large bowl and toss to combine. Combine remaining ingredients and pour over shrimp mixture; cover and marinate overnight or as long as 2 days, stirring occasionally. To serve, drain mixture thoroughly and serve on shredded crisp lettuce.

Yield: 10 appetizer or first-course servings

Opening night at The Beehive was like a Hollywood premiere with all the major film personalities and studio executives turned out in full panoply. They came by invitation only and the expensive invitations were heavy black cards embossed with gold lettering and an elegant queen bee. The Estabrook operation commanded a hillside view of Los

Angeles and the whole cinema city, but many a guest never looked beyond the gardens, which were a landscaped dream. On three sides of the house bougainvillea and wisteria trailed from latticed bowers and there were magnificent magnolias and coco plumosis palms interspersed with color-cued patterns of flowers.

The third-floor bar made a special bow to the movie colony with rows of champagne magnums whose huge corks were the heads and faces of screen greats. The chief bartender was a fat, black man from Baton Rouge, Louisiana. Bee said he looked and acted like he might have been sent over by central casting: "His skin was like polished graphite and he was a wizard with juleps and absinthe frappes."

The Beehive menu continued the honey bee theme, with dishes like the ones that follow.

4 cups chopped, washed and peeled fresh fruit
½ cup dry white wine
¼ cup honey
¼ teaspoon curry powder
Thin slice fresh ginger
Fresh mint leaves, for garnish

Place fruit in a 1½-quart serving dish. Mix remaining ingredients together and pour over the fruit. Cover and refrigerate for several hours. Stir, and garnish with fresh mint before serving.

Yield: 6 servings

The Beehive had an enormous payroll, providing generous income to a huge staff. There were performers (musicians, singers, and comedians), housekeepers, maids, chefs, cooks, waiters, waitresses, porters, laundresses, and a substantial security force made up of hefty private patrolmen. The stars of the staff were the hostesses—eighteen in residence, augmented by a large file of standbys. The file catalogued men as well as women, on call around the clock.

Like Beverly's first house at Belmore, The Beehive catered to both sexes. The Queen Bee herself, as previously mentioned, was bisexual, ready for any kink or quirk. She saw no reason, she said, to rule out a whole sex! Still, she

> **HONEY BUTTER**
>
> This was popular at *The Beehive* as a breakfast spread. Try it!
> ½ cup sweet butter* at room temperature
> 2 tablespoons honey
> In a small bowl, beat butter and honey together until fluffy. Cover and refrigerate. Honey butter keeps well for weeks.
> *Note: Sweet butter is often labeled unsalted butter and is readily available in grocery stores.*
>
> **Yield: 2/3 cup**

strictly forbade lesbian liaisons among her girls, on grounds that it caused jealous fights.

She had learned this the hard way, having once kept a girl in a luxurious apartment "just like a mistress." Without warning, she callously sold a half interest in the girl and the apartment to another madam. Unfortunately, the kept creature was in love with Beverly and was desolated by the arrangement. After brooding about it and drinking all day, she armed herself with one of Beverly pistols, took a cab to the madam's famous club, and forthwith shot up the place. She was shooting at the Queen Bee but was too drunk to hit the intended target. The distraught girl was quietly disarmed and given money to get out of town.

"A lot of girls in the business become lesbians," Beverly said, "because they get rough treatment from men. Like everybody else they want some loving kindness in their lives and what john is going to give that to a whore? He's paying so he's calling the shots and you can't expect him to give a damn about how she feels about anything. So the girls turn to each other for a little tenderness and when one of them falls in love there's hell to pay if her partner doesn't. They fight over each other like men fight over women and usually the madam has to fire both girls. Probably the third one in the triangle, too, and maybe several others. That's why I like to hire girls who don't give a damn about love—the tough little tarts who are there only to make money."

Although so many madams have been wondrously inventive in creating an atmosphere of luxury and fantasy—or homeliness and comfort—theirs is not a pretty profession and, as Beverly herself frequently said, "it's nothing you'd want your sister to get into."

Following is a descendant of 24 Carat Carrots, a recipe that delighted The Beehive customers. Southern California is an agribusiness paradise, with a climate conducive to bumper crops of fruits, vegetables, and millionaire growers. One of the state's best vegetable crops is carrots. Although Hollywood denizens traditionally prefer carats to carrots, this ingenuous vegetable preparation takes the everyday carrot and elevates it to gourmet status.

24 Carat Carrots

1 package (1 pound)
    carrots, peeled and
    cut into ¼-inch
    rounds
⅓ cup mayonnaise
1 tablespoon
    horseradish
1 teaspoon fennel
    seed, crushed
Salt and pepper to
    taste

In a large saucepan,
cook carrots in
enough water to
cover until tender-
crisp; drain. Add
remaining ingredients and toss to coat. Serve immediately.

Yield: 8 servings

California has often been credited with Caesar salad, but this international perennial actually originated across the border in Tijuana, where an Italian immigrant made the salad famous by serving it in his string of restaurants. Mexico was a popular weekend getaway for the Hollywood crowd. Always on the lookout for the new and wonderful, Californians took the idea back to L.A., where it took off. There it quickly made the menu of such notable restaurants as Chasen's and Romanoff's, and now Caesar salad can be found on menus all over the U.S.A. It was once voted the "greatest recipe to originate from the Americans in fifty years" by a prestigious French culinary society. Yes, the name of the creator was Caesar—Caesar Cardini. And here's the way we like his namesake:

Caesar Salad

1 clove garlic, peeled
1 teaspoon dry mustard
1 tablespoon lemon juice
Tabasco sauce to taste
3 tablespoons olive oil
3 heads romaine, washed, patted dry, and torn into bite-
   sized pieces
1 tablespoon freshly grated Parmesan cheese
1 small can anchovies, drained*
1 egg, boiled for 1 minute
1/3 cup croutons
Salt and pepper to taste

Rub a large wooden salad bowl with the garlic. Add
mustard, lemon juice, and Tabasco, stirring until combined.
Add olive oil and whisk until the mixture is blended.
Immediately add romaine, Parmesan, and anchovies, and
break the egg over the salad. Mix gently but thoroughly.
Add croutons and toss to distribute evenly. Season with salt
and pepper to taste. Serve immediately.

Yield: 6 servings

Note: Anchovies were not among the original ingredients. If you choose to
omit them, add some Worcestershire sauce to bring up the flavor of the salad.

7 THE WHORE WITH A HEART OF GOLD

The early movies had it all wrong. The gospel according to MGM held that, except for the villainous outlaws, cowboys were a band of Dudley Do Rights—clean-cut, clean-shaven, clean-living stalwarts who only loved their horses. And every whore blessed the West with a heart of gold! Also, while the movies were awash with likker—always gulped straight before the showdown shoot-out—almost nobody was ever seen eating. Food seldom caught a film director's attention, although many of our enduringly popular foods can trace their origins to the open plains.

Beef jerky, a snack enjoyed by today's hikers and backpackers, was a staple with early Western pioneers because it was light, easy to tote, and kept almost indefinitely. Eventually, this salty but flavorful, high-protein product made its way to the saloons of the West, where it can still be found as a bar snack. And it's available, too, in many supermarkets and specialty food stores.

Dried beans were another everyday stand-by in the early West, popular also with our current crop of young adventurers. Aware or not of their high-protein content, cowboys packed them because they were cheap, filling, and easy to cook. A good thing because animal protein along the trail was often scarce. Since beans are also a rich source of calcium, phosphorous, and iron, all a cowboy needed to do to fix himself a fortifying meal was catch water from the stream, add it to the beans, and cook them over his campfire.

Rice was another food item that found its way into the saddlebags of the wild West. And it was rice that provided the rare dish that even vaguely resembled a dessert. The cowboys often carried raisins and when they tossed a handful of them into a pot of rice boiling away in creek water, they had a primitive version of rice pudding.

The Denver sandwich, more to modern tastes and enjoyed now cross-country, originated "out West" in the mining area around its namesake. This classic dish begins with a scrambled egg. While it cooks, you add chopped ham, onion, and green pepper—and serve it on bread, toast, or a roll. By the way, cowboys never mentioned food; it was "grub."

In his illustrated history, *Great Bordellos of the World*, Emmet Murphy observed that "not until the present decade have film-makers recognized the fact of the symbiotic relationship between cowboys and the cheapest whores."

Murphy shatters one popular illusion by pointing out that Calamity Jane, who has been romantically portrayed in movies and television by some of our most glamorous stars, was actually the hard-bitten transvestite daughter of a prostitute. Jane not only worked in bawdy houses herself but patronized the places disguised as a man. She eventually operated a house of her own and, according to Murphy, was called Calamity not so much in recognition of her skills as a rough and tumble frontier scout, but to describe the consequences of a visit to her bedrooms. She was undeniably one of the wildest women in the West, a confirmed alcoholic at twenty-four, and an all-round hell-raiser who was peerless at driving a bull team (oxen) with a thirty-foot bullwhacker's whip.

Confusing her sexual identity still further was Jane's schoolgirlish crush on Wild Bill Hickok, who dressed in fancy buckskins and was said to be much prettier than she was—his flourishing mustache notwithstanding. The mustache, in fact, was another element of beauty in those days. When Wild Bill was shot and killed, Calamity Jane began fantasizing that he had been her doting lover and went into mourning that lasted until her own death at age fifty-one. Deadwood, her sympathetic hometown in the Dakota territory, treated her to the most flamboyant funeral the Badlands had ever seen and buried her beside her beloved Wild Bill. Although Bill had never loved her, he always considered her a friend, and Deadwood figured he wouldn't mind her graveyard company.

A main dish served after funerals and at other large gatherings back then was a concoction called sonofabitch stew. Its basis was the available game—jack rabbit, squirrel, deer, buffalo, elk, moose, 'possum, even rattlesnake, or bear. These, singly or in any combination, were cooked for hours with potatoes, onions, and additions of whatever else was handy. And "Cookie" (the name always applied by the movies to the ranch cook, wagon train cook, or miner's camp cook) used a lot of creativity in his effort to keep those Western hombres from killing him. Even if they were entirely satisfied with the grub Cookie served them, it was against the code of the plains to admit it, and no meal was considered complete until the poor man's life had been thoroughly and colorfully threatened.

We present here our own version of Cookie's most famous dish, refined now in both name and content. It's hearty fare for any large, hungry gathering.

S.O.B. Stew

½ cup flour
½ teaspoon ground cloves
½ teaspoon ground allspice
½ teaspoon ground cinnamon
½ teaspoon black pepper
4 pounds beef rump or chuck,
    cut into 1½-inch cubes
½ cup butter
3 cups water
1 beef bouillon cube
1 bay leaf
½ cup bourbon
5 dashes of Angostura bitters
8 to 10 carrots, peeled and cut into 2-inch pieces
10 to 12 small potatoes, scrubbed
6 to 8 small onions, peeled and halved
Salt to taste

In a plastic bag, combine flour, cloves, allspice, cinnamon, and pepper. Add beef, a little at a time, shaking to coat pieces on all sides. Continue until all the meat is coated.

Melt butter in a heavy skillet or Dutch oven; add meat, a few pieces at a time, and cook until lightly browned, removing browned pieces as you add floured ones. Cook until all the meat is browned. Return all the meat to the pan and add the water, bouillon cube, and bay leaf. Cover and simmer over low heat for about 1½ hours. Add the bourbon and bitters, stirring to combine. Add carrots, potatoes, and onion, cover, and cook until meat and vegetables are tender, about 45 minutes.

Yield: 8 to 12 servings

Stew, both a noun and a verb, is an interesting culinary word. As a noun, it means a thick, soup-like mixture that most often contains both meat and vegetables to make a complete meal. The verb denotes

THE BORDELLO COOKBOOK

the cooking method—slow cooking in a tightly covered pot, which serves to blend the flavors and tenderize the meat. The West's blunt sonofabitch stew traditionally used meats that were as tough as the baddies they were named for. Many of them were extremely flavorful— if stewed—and the same can be said for today's cheaper cuts of beef in our S.O.B. offering. Another tidbit about this historic stew: It must contain some booze. You know, the meat gets "stewed" in yet another way.

Of all the colorful legends spawned in the great wild West, few have logged more mileage than "the whore with a heart of gold." You've heard the fable sung, seen it danced, and watched it rerun countless times on late-night television. The heroine celebrated in all these performances was a loose lady, for sure. But, according to the script, she was also a creature of kindness and courage, the like of which her world had never dreamed. Never mind that some of her sisters in vice might have had no heart at all. The theme goes on. And on...

The heart-of-gold-whore legend could have been born in the Idaho Territory, where the gold strike touched off a stampede of loose ladies, among them a flashy, young beauty who became known as Molly b'DAM. She arrived in Murray, Idaho, as Molly Burdan (accent on the last syllable) and her entrance was spectacular even for an area that knew few restraints. Molly rode her stallion into a saloon at full gallop and, without dismounting, ordered drinks for the whole house. When she introduced herself to one of the impressed drunks as Molly Bur-Dan, he misunderstood and announced to the crowd that the new girl in town was Molly b'DAM.

The fascinating newcomer explained that she wouldn't be needing hotel accommodations because she planned to take over cabin number one. Throughout the West, cabin number one was reserved for the reigning madam and, since Molly's looks and style were immediately appreciated, she was gallantly helped down from her horse and made welcome. The drunk's name for her stuck and for miles around she became famed as Molly b'DAM.

Molly fell in love with the tough mining town and quickly established herself both as a talented madam and the local "angel of

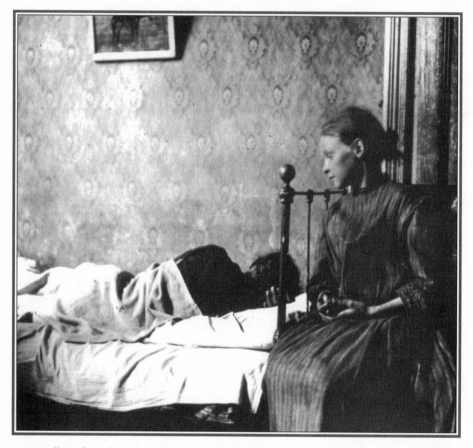

mercy." In her book called *Soiled Doves—Prostitution in the Early West*, Anne Seagraves wrote that the beautiful young madam was kind to her girls and kindly to the whole community, habitually seeking out and feeding hungry families. "Anyone who was down on their luck," Seagraves said, "knew that Molly b'DAM would provide warm clothing and shelter. Although she lived in luxury, Molly never hesitated to climb to a mountain cabin to nurse a sick prospector." Seagraves also reported that in 1886 a stranger arrived in Murray with a burning fever, made his way on horseback to a saloon where he promptly downed a pint of whiskey, and just as promptly dropped dead. The man had smallpox and suddenly the whole town was at risk. "Soon people began dying by the dozens," Seagraves wrote. "They tried to hide in their houses, hoping it would pass them by but it never did. There was one ineffectual doctor in town and no hospital and everyone was terrified."

THE BORDELLO COOKBOOK

The situation became critical and Molly b'DAM called a town meeting. In high fury, she berated the people for holing up in their houses, shunning their stricken neighbors who were dying alone and unattended. "Well, I'm not afraid," she shouted. "There are a dozen sick men up there in my part of town and me and my girls are doing what we can for them."

Molly's fire-breathing speech stirred the town into action. Under her brisk direction they cleared out the hotels and filled them with patients who were then faithfully attended by Molly, the prostitutes who worked for her, and other townspeople who had been shamed into helping their desperately ill neighbors. Molly worked tirelessly, often without time-out to eat or change clothes, and her exhaustion was said to have cost her her life. She developed consumption and "wasted away," dying at age thirty-five. Although this was the end of Molly, it was the beginning of a hundred B movies and television scripts about the whore with a heart of gold. And Molly b'DAM continues to inspire stories of courage and sacrifice by unvirtuous women of the early West who defied death to help others.

Molly b'DAM's Chicken Soup

Molly and her girls made gallons of chicken soup for their stricken neighbors—the soup we now know as "Jewish penicillin," because a million Jewish mothers have enshrined it as both culinary delight and household remedy. Chicken soup remains the first course at dinner on Jewish holidays and the first thought for anybody who so much as sneezes. Here's the simplest chicken soup in the world, the all-time champion. You can, of course, add anything to it that you like, but here is the basic recipe—so tried and true that we name it in honor of our original heart-of-gold heroine.

6 to 8-pound stewing hen

3 quarts water

2 onions

3 carrots, pared and cut into 2-inch pieces

½ cup fresh parsley

6 whole peppercorns

Place all ingredients in a large stockpot with a loose-fitting cover. Bring to a boil, lower heat to a simmer, and cook for 2 hours, skimming occasionally. Remove from the heat and let the hen cool in the broth. Remove the hen to a platter and strain the soup, discarding the vegetables. Refrigerate the soup for several hours or overnight. Remove the hardened fat that has formed on the surface. Reheat the soup and serve garnished with fresh dill and/or parsley, if desired.

Yield: 3 quarts

Note: Use the meat from the chicken for a salad or a casserole.

Prostitution was big business all over the West and in some places it was practically an industry. One such was Helena, which in 1875 was officially named capital of the Montana Territory, although it had yet to become an incorporated city. The historian Paula Petrik cites Helena's many prospering madams as "Capitalists with Rooms." According to Petrik, approximately 60 percent of the madams reported either personal wealth or property—or both!—and over half of Helena's prostitutes had sound finances. One of the most prosperous was a woman known from New York to Nevada as Chicago Joe. As her name implied, she had won her spurs (so to speak) in Chicago, where she learned that it is more blessed at the bank to be a madam than just one of the girls.

She also learned that serving food and drink was an added attraction for any house and in the Montana Territory her many houses became famous for Slumgullion—a noble creation for an area where culinary ingredients were scarce. Slumgullion was a term used by the Western miners for a makeshift food or drink, but Chicago Joe's kitchens turned it into an art. Following is our interpretation of the dish.

Note: One of the reasons why we call this recipe Slumgullion is that you can substitute ingredients you have on hand. For instance, the 3 cups of beef could be shredded leftover roast beef that you cooked yourself or bought at the deli for sandwiches. Of course, you can start with fresh ground beef cooked especially for this dish. Or maybe use leftover chicken or turkey. Many lingering vegetable tidbits can be added along with the chili beans and chiles. Let your creative juices be your guide. We've added mushrooms, peas, celery, and sweet peppers that have been lurking in the fridge for a day or so. Just be sure to avoid vegetables with too strong a flavor, like broccoli, cauliflower, or cabbage.

Slumgullion

3 cups cooked beef (see note above)
1 can (15¾ ounce) chili beans in chili sauce
1 can (4 ounce) chopped green chiles
1 medium onion, chopped
½ teaspoon ground cumin
½ teaspoon Worcestershire sauce
1 package (8½ ounce) corn muffin mix
1 cup shredded sharp Cheddar cheese
Fresh cilantro, for garnish

Preheat the oven to 425°F.

In a medium bowl, combine beef, chili beans, green chiles, onion, cumin, and Worcestershire Sauce. Set aside. Prepare cornbread according to package directions; put batter into greased 9-inch-square pan. Spoon beef mixture over batter, leaving a 1-inch border all around. Bake for 25 minutes, until lightly browned. Add shredded cheese to top and continue baking for another 5 minutes. Remove and let stand for 5 to 10 minutes before serving.

Yield: 8 to 10 servings

Lured by reports of the mining riches rampant in Montana, at age twenty-three, Chicago Joe caught the train to Helena and set up shop there in a ramshackle "hurdy-gurdy" house. The ramshacklery hardly mattered. In three years, the canny madam had made so much money that empire-building was the obvious next step.

The expansion she had in mind required capital and to get it (from Helena's toughest usurer) she mortgaged everything she had, including her underwear. Her contract with the demanding lender actually listed among items posted for security "three dozen pairs of underclothes." It was worth the risk—from the skin out. By the time she was thirty, Chicago Joe was the largest landowner on flourishing Wood Street, heart of the local demimonde. She was owner and operator of several flourishing brothels, all serving better meals than anything available in most of Helena's restaurants, including the pretentious hotel dining rooms.

Helena's lively new sex empress was an immigrant who had arrived in New York at age fourteen, penniless, having left her native Ireland to escape poverty. New York provided no escape, until she discovered the market value of sex. In an effort to trade up, she changed her name from plain Mary Welch to one that, to her, exuded ladylike elegance—Josephine Airey—only to have it vulgarized by her sisters in vice to Chicago Joe, with a masculine "e."

Chicago Joe became one of the most prominent women in the Montana Territory—wealthy, powerful, fashionable—a generous supporter of local charities and civic enterprises. She built a huge entertainment center called the Coliseum, a theater, and "variety house" where the variety was, indeed, infinite. The place was lavishly furnished and equipped with unusual amenities. In the theater, for instance, special boxes were equipped with electric bells that signaled the bar for whatever a gentleman's heart desired: from food and drink to an accommodating female companion.

Something sure to "ring them bells" for refreshments at the theater would be our refreshing switch on coffee with booze:

Almond Iced Coffee

> 1 cup strong coffee, cooled
> 1 cup milk
> 1 jigger almond liqueur
> Sugar to taste
> Ice cubes
> Pinch of unsweetened cocoa powder
>
> Combine coffee, milk, almond liqueur, and sugar. Pour over ice cubes. Dust the top with cocoa.

Yield: 2 servings

It was great fun while it lasted, but the curtain fell on Joe's theater, the whole Coliseum, and practically everything else in her overwrought empire. Like so many other tycoons of the day, Chicago Joe was wiped out by the financial panic of 1893. She lost everything except her cherished Red Light Saloon, which had been her take-off point. She and her husband, a one-time Chicago gambler named Al Hankins, moved into an apartment above the saloon and lived there quietly until Joe died of pneumonia at age fifty-six. The West was inclined to be generous to the departed and gave Joe a rousing send-off, an elaborate funeral marked by fulsome eulogies for the poor little immigrant girl who came to America penniless and left in almost the same condition, but in the interim had been an empress.

At most funerals, then the same as now, there was prodigious eating and drinking. Food and refreshments were brought by the people who gathered to pay their respects. The "bring a dish" custom, still observed in many places, is a food phenomenon that has no strict regional origin but was particularly common in the early West. Maybe it's because people had to stick together in order to survive. They willingly helped each other with everything from building cabins to burying the dead. Hardship and adversity were constant and on occasions of mourning or celebration everybody pitched in. Women brought a dish and men brought a jug, a keg, or a bottle.

Colorado, in settlement days, attracted some of the most interesting shady ladies in the country, and the miners pursuing their fortunes there pro-duced memorable dog-gerel on the subject.

One enduring quatrain contributed by the Colorado Historical Society in Denver was this tender tombstone tribute:

> **Here lies the body of Virginia Marlotte, She was born a virgin and died a harlot. For 18 years she preserved her virginity. That's a damned good record for this vicinity!**

The Society has no historical data on Virginia Marlotte, but we feel that any woman deemed worthy of a rhymed epitaph deserves the approbation of a recipe with her name on it. We serve this one when we entertain our Denver friends and they love it.

Orange Salad Marlotte

6 navel oranges, including zest, peeled and sliced
1 cup salt-cured black olives, halved and pitted
½ cup minced fresh parsley
½ cup minced scallions
1 clove garlic, minced
2 tablespoons olive oil
½ teaspoon ground cumin
½ teaspoon dried oregano
2 tablespoons olive oil
Bibb lettuce, optional

In a large bowl, combine all ingredients, except the Bibb lettuce. Cover and refrigerate for a few hours or overnight.

THE BORDELLO COOKBOOK

To serve, spoon into Bibb lettuce cups, if desired.

Yield: 4 to 6 servings

Note*: To make a small meal of it, serve this salad accompanied by sharp Cheddar or Parmesan cheese straws or a small disc of chèvre and a cracker or roll.*

One of the real winners on record at the Colorado Historical Society is Poker Alice, who was born in England, the daughter of a respectable school teacher. Her parents moved to America, where she was educated in a Southern girls' school and brought up to be a proper lady. The ladyship idea went over the rainbow when Alice married a mining engineer whose work took the couple to Lake City, Colorado. There was nothing much to do in Lake City but play cards in the local saloon and Alice tried her hand at the going pastime with agreeable results. She was lucky and she was good, habitually winning a great deal more than she lost.

When her husband was killed in a mining accident, she had to support herself, and her facility at cards opened up an extraordinary career opportunity. When Lake City began closing down for the winter, Alice moved to other towns where she made an agreeable living playing faro and stud poker. In New Mexico her fame flashed across the entire West when she broke the bank at a gaming house in twenty-seven hours of straight stud.

HAM LOAF (THREE OF A KIND*)

Alice won the last hand with "three of a kind"—three tens—which beat the two pairs held by the house. The following supper dish is named for her triumph:

1 cup fresh bread crumbs
1 pound ground smoked ham
1 pound ground pork
½ cup sweet pickle relish
1 cup milk
2 eggs
1 tablespoon Dijon mustard
1 teaspoon ground ginger
Salt and pepper to taste

Preheat oven to 350°F.

In a medium bowl, combine bread crumbs, ham, pork, and pickle relish. In another bowl, whisk together remaining ingredients, pour over meat mixture, and mix thoroughly. Transfer to a shallow baking pan and shape into a loaf. Bake for 1 hour.

Yield: 8 servings

"Three of a Kind" in culinary terms refers to a dish that can be served equally well in three ways. Such is this devilish ham concoction: serve it hot, as a dinner entrée; cut room temperature slices for a grand sandwich; crumble or cube the remainder into a mixture of salad greens for a super maindish salad.

After Alice's bank-breaking feat, no gaming house in New Mexico was eager to give her a seat at the table and she moved on to Deadwood, Colorado. There she married W. G. Tubbs, a gambler whose life she had saved when another gambler pulled a knife on him. (Alice simply whipped a pistol out of her reticule and plugged the knifer with a single, well-placed shot.) The marriage didn't last long because Tubbs caught pneumonia and died. A blizzard prohibited his burial for several days, which was all to the good because it gave Alice time to hock her wedding ring to pay for his burial. An unaccustomed run of bad luck at the tables had made the hocking necessary for her but after the funeral Alice promptly won the ring back along with a sizable stack of cash.

She then moved to Sturgis where, in a long winning streak at seven-card stud, she became known as Poker Alice. The black cigars she always chewed became her trademark and her winning ways continued. She opened her own gambling place and, with a nod to her education, announced that there were *nymphs du pavé* (girls of the pavement) for entertainment. The miners didn't know what *nymphs du pavé* meant but they knew what the girls were there for anyway and acted accordingly.

Alice remained very religious. She closed her operation down on Sundays and made the girls attend church, hatted, gloved, and otherwise modestly attired. Although she didn't really want another husband, she married a third time after an employee named Heckert badgered her for weeks with proposals. Heckert was her bartender—

"the only one I ever had who didn't steal me blind." Alice eventually gave in and married him, only after she realized that she owed him $1,000 in back wages. She decided that, for the moment anyway, it was cheaper to marry him than pay him off.

Since Alice had already had two honeymoons, she saw no reason to squander hard-won money on a third. To celebrate, she simply cooked a wedding supper for Heckert and their best saloon customers. The menu consisted of roast suckling pig, complete with the apple in its mouth, and all the trimmings. Although most of us would be no more likely to roast a whole suckling pig than we would be to marry a bartender to avoid paying his back wages, it should be remembered that some people still do. (Roast a suckling pig, that is.) All told, Americans consume more than fifty pounds of pork per capita, in some form or other, each year. Bacon remains beloved in spite of the nutritional no-noes and ham is an all-American favorite. The following recipe is special enough for Easter, when ham is the traditional favorite. Still it's easy enough for any family dinner.

Ham Glazed with Apricot Mustard

Friends who have shared this luscious ham with us declare it the best pork dish they've ever eaten, but Poker Alice and her group would no doubt pass it up for suckling pig. She reported that her wedding pig weighed twenty-two pounds and "that pack of drunks ate every bit of it right down to and including the tail."

One 10-pound fully cooked ham, bone in
15 to 20 whole cloves
½ cup apricot jam
½ cup prepared mustard
5 cloves garlic
¼ cup dark brown sugar
1 tablespoon Worchestershire sauce
Preheat oven to 350°F.

Score ham with a sharp knife in a grid pattern. Stud with cloves to decorate. Place ham in a large roasting pan.

Combine remaining ingredients in food processor and process until smooth; spread evenly over top and sides of ham. Bake for 1 hour, basting occasionally with pan juices.

Yield: 6 to 8 servings

Meanwhile, silver-rich Denver was in a fever of excitement—nowhere more than on Market Street, which had been largely taken over by the prospering "landladies" and saloon keepers. The new girls in town usually headed straight for Market, originally known as Holladay Street, because they knew they could always find work there. There were many sad tales on the street. Some of the girls were from respectable families who shed their real identity along with their scruples when they swapped respectability for the glitter and glitz of hell-raising Denver.

Market Street even had its own Romeo and Juliet, a pair of star-crossed lovers whose romance had a final curtain that was tragic enough for Shakespeare. She was a young bordello beauty whose working name was Lois Lovell and he was a socially prominent young Denver businessman whose first visit to her was made on a bet. He won both the bet and Lois—all of her! Suddenly the two were desperately in love and the smitten young gentleman was begging Lois to marry him. She refused on grounds that his marriage to a Market Street girl would destroy him socially and professionally. "I love you too much to marry you," she sobbed, whereupon her broken-hearted lover left town on a long, lonely business trip, bitterly determined to try to forget her.

The story goes that Lois knew he was leaving Denver on a train at ten minutes past noon. Locking herself in her room, she watched the

clock until the hands reached 12:10. At that precise moment she swallowed poison and shortly afterward died. Meanwhile, the young man relented. He worked out an elaborate plan by which he could begin a new career in a faraway city where they would start a new life together, married and undiscussed. He rushed home to tell her the news and when he heard of her death went straight to the cemetery where she was buried and shot himself dead at her grave.

Melodramatic fiction? The wild old West was full of it. And some of it was true. But true or not, the stories go on and on. So does Denver's Market Street—once the red-light district of a raucous, ragtag, mining town, but now one of the many delights in the beloved Mile High City. The street today is a strip of themed restaurants, coffee bars, trendy pubs, and fancy shops catering to cool, young Denverites and streams of fascinated tourists. Several of the old parlor houses have actually been converted to apartment houses whose history gives them added cachet.

Cheese Chips / Market Street

In Denver, recently, we picked up an idea for these crispy little cocktail tidbits that are much too chic for the area as it was "back when." We salute today's fashion-conscious Market Street with our version of the recipe:

1 cup flour
½ teaspoon salt
¼ teaspoon baking powder
5 tablespoons butter
1 cup shredded sharp Cheddar cheese
3 tablespoons water
½ teaspoon hot paprika

In a large mixing bowl, combine flour, salt and baking powder, cut in butter until mixture resembles coarse meal. Stir in shredded cheese; sprinkle water over mixture while tossing with a fork. Using your hands, pack mixture together to form 2 logs about 3 inches in diameter. Wrap cheese logs in plastic wrap and refrigerate several hours or overnight. Preheat oven to 425°F.

Cut cheese logs into ¼ inch rounds and sprinkle sparingly with hot paprika. Bake on cookie sheets until golden, about 10 minutes. Remove to a cooling rack and when cool store these chippies in an airtight container to keep them crisp. Enjoy them with a cocktail or a glass of wine.

Yield: About 40 chips

There are interesting ghost towns in the nearby mountains, and Denver itself is a city of incredible ghosts who still haunt the booming metropolis. Denver holds amusing memories of the show-off vulgarians who dominated the place in the early twentieth century. Characters like Denver's "unsinkable Molly Brown" who saved a lifeboat full of terrified people fleeing the foundering *Titanic*. And the city's Silver King, H.A.W. Tabor, who married legendary Baby Doe and, to please her, bought one hundred live peacocks to decorate their lawn. The peacocks drowned in a rainstorm, "Haw" died broke, and Baby Doe froze to death guarding Haw's defunct silver mine, the once world-famous "Matchless." The unsinkable Molly Brown died with her jewelry on, still rich, still roaring, and eventually memorialized in a long-running Broadway show followed by a movie.

But few women have left behind richer memories than Jennie Rogers who was crowned "Denver's Immoral Queen" by the author, Caroline Bancroft. In *Six Racy Madams of Colorado*, Bancroft wrote that the red-light district in Denver in 1879 was already sensational, but the arrival of Jennie Rogers created "a new and larger sensation."

Bancroft described her as "a flashingly beautiful wild one." Among other things, Jennie was a daredevil horsewoman who enjoyed dashing through the streets on horseback or careening around corners in a four-in-hand coach. Her reckless horseback riding once caused her to be arrested for "unladylike behavior in the streets," but her demeanor under other circumstances was said to be dignified and proper. Apparently, horses drove her crazy or, at least, stirred up some strong animal instincts.

The new madam bought a two-story brick parlor house at 2009 Market Street from Mattie A. Silks who, according to Bancroft, was at the time queen of the business in Denver. Jennie quickly out-queened her. Within a few years her clientele had grown so large that she needed new quarters, and in 1884 built the largest, most lavish parlor house in the area. It was a lofty, three-story structure with three reception rooms, a ballroom, dining room, and kitchen on the first floor and fifteen bedrooms on the two floors above. In the basement were a well-stocked wine cellar, huge storage closets, and servants quarters.

Jennie's girls and the johns who chose to dine with them ate well. A substantial, brunch-like meal was served in the middle of the day and there was an early dinner. The food was delicious and fortifying. It had to be robust because the girls needed to keep their strength up. Jennie's last grocery bills listed chickens, steaks, roasts, cheeses, milk, cream, fresh vegetables, fresh fruit, and a number of unlikely delicacies. The madam was a sharp manager, but nobody ever said she was stingy. Oddly, lamb is not on her grocery list, a surprise to us because so much of today's American lamb is raised next door on the Rocky Mountain grasslands.

For this omission, we apologize to our friends who grow and market these tender creatures and present here our favorite lamb entrée:

Roast Saddle of Lamb

1 saddle of lamb, trimmed (about 1 pound)
1 tablespoon olive oil
1 teaspoon freshly ground black pepper
1 teaspoon paprika
½ teaspoon ground coriander
½ cup fine dried bread crumbs
¼ cup chopped fresh parsley
¼ cup mint leaves
2 cloves minced garlic
1 teaspoon mustard seeds
Salt to taste

Preheat oven to 400°F.

Place lamb in roasting pan. Combine olive oil, pepper, paprika, and coriander and rub mixture into surface of the lamb. Roast for about 15 minutes.

In a food processor, combine remaining ingredients. When lamb has roasted, spread crumb mixture on top, return to oven, and roast for another 7 to 10 minutes, or until coating is crisp. Remove lamb to rest for a few minutes before slicing thin. Serve immediately.

Yield: 4 servings

The 1880s were turbulent for Jennie. Unfortunately, the existing public records are so garbled that it's difficult to isolate significant details. What is known for sure is that she owned, leased, and operated many houses, was arrested, tried, and fined many times and inspired the most contradictory stories that this writer has ever researched. One of her most famous places of business was her House of Mirrors, so called because the parlor opening off the reception hall was completely mirror-lined. Caroline Bancroft says that a crystal chandelier hung from a large circular mirror on the ceiling. "The whole effect," she wrote, "was of a sparkling lightness that glittered in a manner completely foreign to the usual heaviness and darkness of Victorian parlors, respectable or otherwise."

The House of Mirrors was countered by Jennie's grotesque "house of carved heads," said to be an architectural allegory for a weird scandal that erupted around Jennie. The scandal was too confused to report but the building itself is describable. It had a greystone facade with four "plain, somewhat phallic pillars" rising along the roof line. At the base of the pillars are four gargoyle-like faces carved in rose stone: "two men, an old woman and possibly a fat boy" says Bancroft. Above them all is a sculptured face of (who else?) Jennie Rogers. Or did someone sneak in a substitute—a sculpture, perhaps, of her beautiful

The Bordello Cookbook

biographer, Caroline Bancroft? Many people have declared Bancroft "a dead ringer" for the radiant young Jenny—a really astonishing look-alike.

Although Bancroft, who wrote many books on Western history, kept her slim figure and artfully chiseled features, Jennie's profession took its toll. In her later years she became heavy-bodied and gross but, thanks to her biographer, the West still remembers the dashing young figure she cut as "Denver's Immoral Queen."

8 TEXAS FOREVER!

If "The Best Little Whorehouse in Texas" really was the best that the state had to offer, it triumphed over some formidable competition.

First of all, Fort Worth. Around the turn of the century, Fort Worth was called "The Paris of the Prairie." Most of the people who called it that had never seen Paris or anything else east of the Mississippi River but never mind. Rootin', tootin' Fort Worth was the home of Hell's Half Acre, a roaring red-light district loaded with saloons, gaming tables, and assorted other cultural icons. Richard F. Selcer, author of *Hell's Half Acre, the Life and Legend of a Red-light District*, wrote that the city was enormously proud of its wild-and-woolly nature. Several other Texas bastions of vice were apparently more boastful than apologetic about their favorite pastimes—among them San Antonio, Galveston, Austin, and El Paso. These cowtowns were, according to Selcer, Fort Worth's chief rivals for Sin Capital of the State. The author slyly adds this: "Dallas, some Fort Worthers were proud to point out, wasn't even in the running."

As most of the uncivilized world knows by now, "The Best Little Whorehouse in Texas" was the globally acclaimed Chicken Ranch, so-called because during the Great Depression live chickens were

acceptable currency there. The rate of exchange was one chicken per trick. Flocks of the barterable birds roosted in the nearby trees and their owners fired shotguns into the air all night to discourage Texas A&M boys who habitually went tree climbing to steal the requisite admission fee.

The Chicken Ranch held forth for over twenty years in the belly button of nowhere, just outside La Grange, Texas, which is near Houston, which evidently wasn't in the running for Sin Capital either. In his definitive history of Lone Star prostitution, Selcer mentions Houston only to pin down the location of La Grange. "The Best Little Whorehouse in Texas" has, if anything, been overglorified: in books and magazine articles, in two shows on Broadway (one of which laid an egregious egg), and an ambitious starlit movie starring Dolly Parton, herself. However, there are unsung, even unnamed houses all over Texas

THE Bordello Cookbook

that many a man, without a feather of valid evidence, would swear were far superior to the Chicken Ranch.

Fort Worth had contenders by the dozen. The cowhands and drovers could hardly wait to get there, even though the houses lacked the amenities of sex mansions described elsewhere in this book. The rootless cowboys gravitated naturally to the saloons because that was where they felt at home. Every barkeeper in turn felt it his professional responsibility to provide abundant hospitality, certainly enough to keep the cowboys spending their money there, instead of foraging for food and girls elsewhere. Female companionship was always at the bar and for twenty-five cents most saloons offered a meal of sorts. The menu was posted in whitewash lettering on the mirror behind the bar, and the food wasn't good but it was no worse than the booze. Most of the cowboys couldn't read, which was no real handicap because they could always order ham and beans. The menu never varied from saloon to saloon and the ham and bean special was always on the mirror.

The cowboys didn't have nutrition in mind when they ordered their two-bit meal, but with the beans they got a healthy supply of protein, vitamins A and C, iron, and thiamine—the stuff that makes beans valued by health-conscious people today. Here's a recipe rich in all of the above and unusually good, too:

Beans, Lone Star Saloon Style

> 1 pound dried pink beans, soaked according to package
>   directions
> 3 slices bacon
> 1 onion, chopped
> 2 cloves garlic, minced
> ½ cup chopped green pepper
> 1 lemon, thinly sliced
> 1 can (1 pound) tomatoes, including liquid
> ¼ cup brown sugar
> ¼ cup Worcestershire sauce
> ¼ cup prepared mustard
> 1 teaspoon sweet paprika

1 teaspoon dried oregano
½ teaspoon dried coriander
1 can (12 ounces) beer, divided

Drain beans, set aside. In a large Dutch oven, crisp-fry bacon. Remove, add onion and garlic to bacon fat, and sauté until soft. Add beans, half the beer, and remaining ingredients. Simmer, uncovered for about 30 minutes.

Meanwhile, preheat oven to 325°F. Place bacon strips over the top of the beans. Bake uncovered for 2 hours, checking beans occasionally, adding reserved remaining beer to keep them from drying out. Cover and bake for another two hours or until beans are tender yet firm, adding more beer as needed.

Yield: 6 to 8 servings

A cowboy earned only about $30 a month and he took every cent of it to town the minute he got it. By daybreak the next day, he was flat broke. He was also exhausted, if not injured, and too hungover to remember the fun he'd had. In the interim, his $30 would have been invested in the saloons where he had enjoyed (or, at least, thought he had enjoyed) the girls, gaming tables, grub, killer-whiskey, and music. As for the music, the sign on the piano was serious: "Please don't shoot the piano player—he's doing the best he can."

The Tivoli Hall Saloon offered the best deal in town: a hot lunch served all day to bar customers. The whiskey, like the food, was of regrettable quality. But it was lovingly referred to as rot gut, redeye, tarantula juice, and Who-Hit-John. Beer was available but until refrigeration arrived, around 1900, it was served at room temperature, which, in the Texas summer, was nobody's idea of refreshment. The saloon pets, Selcer said, were as rough as the customers: "One had a half-wild caged wolf, another a panther that once scalped a man." So much for party animals in frontier Fort Worth.

Mop Sauce

One of the great cooking ideas that have come down to us

from the wild frontier is mop sauce. There are many
variations, depending on how your mother made it, which,
in turn, depended on what ingredients she had in the
house. One thing, however, is standard: Every recipe starts
with strong, leftover coffee.

1 cup strong black coffee
½ cup ketchup
½ cup Worcestershire sauce
2 tablespoons olive oil
1 tablespoon molasses
1 teaspoon hot sauce
1 clove garlic, minced.
Salt and pepper to taste

In a small bowl, combine all ingredients, stirring until
smooth. Use as a marinade and sauce for beef, pork, or
poultry.

Yield: 2½ cups

Note*: It's called Mop Sauce because you mop it up with hunks of bread,
rolls, or biscuits—an ideal way to dawdle over a casual, home-cooked meal.*

Fort Worth's attractions reached beyond the $30-a-month cowboys. They also drew in such big-time gamblers as Bat Masterson, Wyatt Earp, and "Doc" Holliday, the gun-toting dentist who was the role model for the doctor in television's famed *Gunsmoke*. It will be recalled that the long-running *Gunsmoke* show romanticized yet another heart-of-gold creature, the much-admired Miss Kitty. In today's more explicit television, Miss Kitty's role would hardly be veiled and glossed over as it was in *Gunsmoke*. In all probability, she would be candidly presented as a generous and kindly madam.

The real "Doc's" stay in Fort Worth was tranquil enough, but he ran into trouble with the law at Fort Griffin, Texas. The records don't show what the trouble was but it must have been serious because he was a carefully guarded guest in the local jail. His faithful girlfriend, Big Nose Kate Fisher, was concerned enough about his future to ride to his rescue. Some people said Kate did it because she was lonely for her favorite man, while others remarked that it was the sort of thing she'd do just for the hell of it. Whatever the reason, she set fire to the local hotel to distract the townspeople and while they were preoccupied with the blaze, saddled two horses and pounded hell-for-leather to the jail. There the robust lady disarmed the terrified guard, unlocked "Doc's" cell with the guard's keys, and the two of them galloped out of town together, laughing all the way.

Neither of the adventurers left behind a diary telling us what they ate that night, but exertion like that calls for a good, revitalizing meal. The next time you and your significant other have had an especially exhausting or frustrating week invite a few close friends over to share this Texas Taco Meat Loaf and be thankful you didn't have to set fire to a hotel to enjoy it. It's the kind of hearty "comfort food" that makes the world go away. Everyone grew up eating meat loaf, but this one is more than a trip down memory lane. The Texas twist gives it a party touch, and if there are leftovers they'll make great sandwiches the next day.

Texas Taco Meat Loaf

1 tablespoon olive oil
½ cup chopped onion
½ cup chopped green pepper
1 pound ground beef
1 pound ground veal
¼ pound ground pork
2 eggs, beaten
1 can (4 ounces) chopped mild green chiles, including
    liquid
½ cup chili sauce
¼ cup fresh cilantro
1 tablespoon chili powder
2 cups taco or tortilla chips

Preheat oven to 350°F.

In a small skillet, heat olive oil, add onion and green peppers, and sauté until softened. In a large bowl, combine meats, mixing lightly. Add the onion mixture, eggs, green chiles and liquid, chili sauce, cilantro, and chili powder. Mix lightly to combine. Place taco or tortilla chips in bowl of food processor. Process to the texture of cornmeal and add to the meat mixture, distributing evenly. Form into a loaf and place in a shallow roasting pan. Bake for 1½ hours.

Yield: 6 to 8 servings

In frontier Fort Worth, three madams were outstanding and any one of them could have been crowned queen of the local trade. They were Mary Porter, Jessie Reeves, and Josie Belmost. The prospering triumvirate competed with each other briskly for the upscale male clientele but, fortunately, the competition was friendly. Their houses were no more than a block apart and while they were always willing to lend each other a cup of sugar (or booze, as the case may be) lending a girl was totally out of the question. There was a tacit understanding among madams about this, so none of the three ever had the poor taste to ask for a loan of the basic merchandise.

They all operated with the acquiescence of the city authorities who were not opposed to prostitution as long as the madams and their freelance sisters paid up. The fees, which were euphemistically called fines, were $13.10 and $9.10, due whenever the officials said they were due. This apparently, happened whenever they felt a need for a bit of extra spending money or when they knew the ladies were enjoying an exceptional run of prosperity. Nobody except "the Do Gooders" complained much about the arrangement between the shady ladies and the city fathers because there was quiet agreement among many citizens that the houses provided a community service.

Selcer wrote that one old-time mayor declared that a town needed at least two houses to keep a level of free enterprise going, and quoted him as saying that competition makes for better conditions in the sporting world. "One parlor house in town," the ex-mayor declared, "is no good."

There are no records of the food served by the Big Three, but the assumption is that it was as extraordinary as the madams were themselves. It had to be to attract and hold top-quality girls and an upscale clientele.

The Bordello Cookbook

Shimmy Sauce was popular in the parlor houses because it was (a) delicious and (b) fun, since it was named for a self-styled "oil witch." Texas and oil have been linked since 1543 when the first petroleum was discovered east of Houston by the Spanish conquistadors. For several hundred years there was no market for the product, but the Machine Age quickly changed that. The oil rigs and the roughnecks who worked the wells became the new American heroes and oil exploration became a Texas preoccupation.

Certain persons claimed the ability to "divine" the presence of underground pools and one was the aforesaid "oil witch." The lady swore that she always began to shimmy uncontrollably when she stepped on ground that had a mother lode of oil below. Let's just say that watching her was more fun than using a divining stick—and so is eating the sauce! The "shimmy" in it is created with the flavorful, slick addition of peanut butter.

4 chicken breasts, boned and skinned
½ cup olive oil, divided
Juice and grated rind of 1 lemon
1 teaspoon dried oregano
¼ cup peanut butter
1 clove garlic
¼ cup chopped cilantro
1 small serrano pepper, seeded
1 teaspoon prepared mustard
1 teaspoon ground cumin

Place chicken breasts in a shallow dish. In a small bowl, combine ¼ cup olive oil, lemon juice, and grated rind, and oregano; rub olive oil mixture evenly over chicken. Cover and refrigerate for at least 1 hour. Place remaining ingredients plus reserved ¼ cup olive oil in food processor and process until smooth and well blended.

Remove chicken from marinade and grill or sauté until golden and juices run clear, adding more marinade to sauté pan or basting chicken with marinade as needed. Serve immediately topped with a drizzle of the shimmy sauce.

Yield: 4 servings

The Spanish influence shows up often in Texas cookery and is evident in the Texas taste for flan. The flavor and consistency of this egg-rich Spanish beauty made Fort Worth's Auntie Olga famous. We can't find anybody who remembers her last name and suspect this dish brought her glory because she added rum, which is not included in the traditional recipe. Typically, it's served with berries in season or orange sections.

Auntie Olga's Famous Flan

1½ cups sugar, divided
¼ cup water
8 eggs
2 (12 ounces each) cans evaporated milk
¼ cup dark rum
Preheat oven to 350°F.

In a small heavy saucepan, combine 1 cup of the sugar and the water over medium heat, stirring constantly until caramel colored. Pour into buttered 1½-quart ring mold or 9 x 5 inch loaf pan, tilting to coat bottom and sides completely; set aside. In a large bowl, beat together the eggs, remaining ½ cup sugar, evaporated milk, and rum. Pour into caramel-coated baking pan. Place flan in a roasting pan large enough to hold flan dish with room to spare. Pour hot water to reach halfway up the sides of the flan dish. Bake for 1 hour, or until a knife inserted in the center comes out clean. Remove flan from the water bath, place on a cooling rack, and cool to room temperature. Cover and refrigerate for 4 to 5 hours or overnight; do not skimp on refrigeration time. To unmold, run the tip of a knife around the edge and invert onto a serving plate with rim. Cut slices or wedges and serve along with fresh berries or fruit, if desired. Refrigerate any leftovers and serve within a day or two.

Yield: 8 to 10 servings

__Note__: If you prefer another flavor, substitute one of the following for the rum:

½ teaspoon vanilla extract

½ teaspoon ground cinnamon

Juice and grated rind of 1 lime

Juice and grated rind of 1 lemon

Mary Porter was the most famous of the three top-seeded Fort Worth madams, probably because she was confused with San Antonio's Fanny Porter. The confusion was in name only because the two Porters could not have been more different. While Mary's house was politically correct in every detail, Fanny's was a hideout for the most lawless men in the West. Fanny was the friend and protector of "The Wild Bunch," the notorious gang of train robbers, horse thieves, and hired killers often portrayed in movies and television shows. They frequently holed up in Fanny's house to plan their daring and over-romanticized robberies. Among the colorful desperadoes who were regulars at Fanny's were Butch Cassidy and the Sundance Kid, handsomely played by Paul Newman and Robert Redford in the famous movie based on the outlaws' crime sprees.

The gang lived "high on the hog" at Fanny's, but when they were pulling a job they ate on the run. Their saddlebags contained such filling fare as sausage biscuits, hard-boiled eggs, cold baked sweet potatoes, and ham sandwiched between slabs of cornbread.

Fanny packed the saddlebags for them and, to wish them luck, served them something special the night before they set out to pull a big job. Nobody ever called it the "last supper," although that was what it turned out to be for some of the gang on several unfortunate occasions. They were aware of the dangers ahead, but you'd never have guessed it from the way they ate and drank.

For Fannie's goodbye-and-good-luck dinners, the grand favorite was barbecued *cabrito*—young goat (a suckling kid), which was cooked in a pit dug into the ground and made into an oven. It's an old Texas custom, still favored among the wealthy ranchers who like to boggle out-of-state visitors with a taste of the colorful past. The next time you're overcome by the urge to barbecue a goat you may want to call up one of your rich friends in Texas and find out exactly how to dig the historic pit and make an oven of it. Or you could control your daring impulses and opt instead for lamb. Here's a modern version of *cabrito*, J. G.'s Lamburgers that require only a barbecue grill for cooking. No need to dig a pit. You can substitute baby goat for the ground lamb if you wish.

J.G.'S Saucy Lamburgers

1½ pounds ground lamb (or goat)
¼ cup chopped cilantro
¼ cup soft goat cheese
Salt and pepper to taste
1 cup plain yogurt
½ cup diced cucumber
1 tablespoon cumin seeds
¼ teaspoon ground cinnamon
¼ teaspoon cayenne pepper

Shape ground meat into 4 patties. In a small bowl, combine cilantro, cheese, and salt and pepper. Make a pocket in the lamb patties and stuff with the cheese mixture, covering the cheese mixture completely with ground meat. Sprinkle with salt and pepper, Grill to desired doneness.

In small bowl, combine remaining ingredients, serve as a sauce to spoon over lamburgers.

Yield: 4 servings

Anyone interested in the lore of Texas bordellos can forget Dallas. The frontier city had a red-light district but little is known of it beyond the fact that it was called Frogtown. A friend who lives there says, "It figures. Dallas is so prim and proper that you can easily understand how people who lived here when the West was wild simply pretended there was no such thing in town as prostitution." The same exists today. Ever since Stanley Marcus brought culture to Texas, the Big D has been trying to live down its uncouth history and has promoted its sophistication.

Whether Le Grand Stanley was responsible for it or not, it must be observed that Dallas has done a pretty good job of burying past indiscretions. The Big D today is one of America's proud cities. It is, indeed, sophisticated, cultivated, and a wonderful place to be hungry. One of the city's many accomplished hostesses is famous for two dishes that are, as she said, "just Western enough." They were the beginnings of these recipes that we enjoy serving to New Yorkers.

"Big D" Ratatouille

2 tablespoons olive oil
1 red onion, chopped
6 cloves garlic, chopped
1 large eggplant, peeled and chopped
1 pound summer squash (zucchini and/or yellow squash), thickly sliced
2 green peppers, seeded and cut into thick strips
½ pound mushrooms, cleaned and halved
¼ cup fresh basil, chopped
¼ cup fresh parsley, chopped
1 teaspoon fresh oregano
1 can (14½ ounces) tomatoes, juice included

Salt and pepper to taste

¼ cup freshly grated Parmesan cheese

In a large skillet, heat oil, add onion, and sauté until soft. Add eggplant and sauté for 8 to 10 minutes, or until just tender. Add remaining ingredients, cover, and simmer for 20 to 30 minutes, until vegetables are tender, stirring occasionally. Top individual servings with Parmesan cheese.

Yield: 6 servings

Note: Ratatouille is often served over polenta, cornbread, or spoon bread. (And, remember, ratatouille is even better next day.)

Lucia's Shrimp and Rice Luncheon Salad

1 cup cooked, peeled and deveined shrimp

1 cup artichoke hearts, canned and drained or frozen (thawed)

2 cups cooked rice, cooled

½ cup chopped scallions

½ cup chopped red peppers

¼ cup toasted pecans, chopped

¼ cup mayonnaise

¼ cup sour cream

Juice of 1 lemon

Salt and pepper to taste

Lettuce (your choice)

Cut shrimp and artichoke hearts into bite-sized pieces, reserving a few for garnish. In a large bowl, combine shrimp, artichokes, rice, scallions, red peppers, and pecans, tossing lightly. In a small bowl, whisk together mayonnaise, sour cream, lemon juice, and salt and pepper; add to rice mixture; toss to coat evenly. Cover and refrigerate for several hours or overnight. Serve on lettuce leaves. Garnish with reserved whole shrimp and artichoke hearts.

Yield: 4 to 6 servings

Beaten Biscuits

Yet another famous Dallas hostess told us she wouldn't dream of having anyone in for cocktails without having a big batch of beaten biscuits ready to serve. They're a grand classic for casual entertaining from Texas all the way over to the Carolinas. Split, spread with honey mustard and, with ham sandwiched between the halves, they're a special favorite of men—particularly the enthusiastic drinkers. The old-fashioned beaten biscuit required a lot of muscle, 200 strokes per batch, but food processors ended the exertion. Give this quick-and-easy recipe a whirl.

2 cups flour
1 teaspoon sugar
½ teaspoon salt
½ teaspoon baking powder
½ cup cold solid vegetable shortening
¼ cup heavy cream
¼ cup ice water

In a food processor, place flour, sugar, salt, and baking powder and process just a couple of seconds to combine. Add shortening and process until mixture resembles coarse meal. With food processor running, add cream and ice water in a steady stream through feed tube. Process until dough forms into a ball, then continue to process another 2 minutes until dough has a sheen.

Preheat oven to 350°F.

Roll dough out onto a lightly floured board to ¼-inch thickness. Fold dough over onto itself to make 2 layers. Cut into 2-inch rounds. Place on an ungreased baking sheet, and prick tops several times with tines of a fork. Bake for 30 minutes, or until biscuits are lightly browned. Serve immediately.

Yield: 2 dozen biscuits

Note: These are also delicious with thin slices of chicken, turkey, or beef. With butter and jam, too!

Meanwhile, thirty miles to the West, Fort Worth remains as proud of its historic wild-and-wooliness as Dallas is of its current sophistication. Since we are inclined to judge all cities with our taste buds, we give high marks to both places—to Fort Worth for a stampede of original dishes with names as colorful and inventive as the foods they describe. One we particularly admire is "Bull's Eye," a visual masterpiece that never fails to mesmerize the cocktail crowd. It's a delightful centerpiece for a buffet or cocktail table: concentric circles of yellow, black, and white centered by a red bull's eye! It looks like something a caterer slaved over for hours, and it's okay to pretend that's what happened. But you can put it together yourself in a few concentrated minutes.

Bull's Eye

(Caviar Cocktail Spread)

2 containers (8 ounces each) whipped cream cheese
2 teaspoons lemon juice
1 jar (2 ounces) red caviar
2 egg yolks, hard cooked
1 jar (4 ounces) black caviar
½ cup finely chopped onion

In a small bowl, cream together cream cheese and lemon juice. Make a "base" for the target by spreading the cream cheese mixture evenly on a 9-inch round, flat serving plate. Use red caviar to make a solid circle (bull's eye) in the center of the cream cheese. Finely crumble the hard-cooked egg yolks and sprinkle in a circle around the red caviar bulls eye. Continue making concentric circles using black caviar and then finely chopped onions. Cover loosely with plastic wrap and refrigerate. Serve with crisp crackers or toast points.

Yield: 12 servings

Note: If there's any of your Bull's Eye extravaganza left (and we doubt there'll be much), just mix it all together and serve it as a caviar-laced cheese ball dip.

THE Bordello Cookbook

Cowboy Caviar

Fort Worth also takes honors for a luscious innovation called "Cowboy Caviar." We served the following version of it to a New York friend who declared it good enough to make him forget beluga. We wouldn't go that far, but it's really delicious—and don't even think about comparative cost!

1 eggplant (about 1½ pounds)
¼ cup olive oil
¼ cup chopped fresh parsley

2 cloves garlic, minced
1 tablespoon lemon juice
1 teaspoon ground cumin
½ teaspoon coarsely ground black pepper
2 tablespoons capers, drained
2 tablespoons chopped pimiento-stuffed olives
Pita bread triangles, for serving

Pierce the eggplant several times with a fork. Place eggplant
in baking dish in microwave oven. Cook on High for 7
minutes, turning once during cooking. When cool, cut
eggplant in half and scoop out flesh; place flesh in food
processor. Purée eggplant and remaining ingredients, except
capers and olives. Chill. Before serving, fold in capers and
olives. Serve with pita bread triangles as dippers.

Yield: 3 cups

Texas Citrus Salad

One of the most refreshing salads we ever ate was a Texas
citrus delight combining fruits of the fabled Rio Grand
Valley. Anyone deluded into the belief that Fort Worth is still
an overgrown cow town should have been at this luncheon,
where the elegant hostess served this with a simple entrée of
broiled chicken breast and Tex-Mex pasta.

2 grapefruits, peeled
2 oranges, peeled
½ cup chopped scallions
¼ cup olive oil
1 tablespoon wine vinegar
½ cup sliced calamata olives
½ cup crumbled feta cheese
Pinch of dried oregano
Salt and pepper to taste

Slice grapefruits and oranges into thin rounds and layer fruit
in a shallow dish. Combine remaining ingredients and
spoon over citrus. Cover and refrigerate for several hours or
overnight.

Yield: 6 to 8 servings

Though it is mentioned nowhere as a candidate for Sin Capital of Texas, Waco turns up with a rich history of prostitution, deftly recorded by one Aimee Harris Johnson. In 1990 Ms. Johnson wrote a thesis titled "Prostitution in Waco," submitting it to the faculty of Baylor University, "in partial fulfillment of the requirements for the degree of Master of Arts."

Waco, originally known as Six Shooter Junction, became a Baptist stronghold identified as "the buckle of the bible belt"—a clasp not strong enough to keep the town from becoming the second in America to legalize prostitution. In an effort to contain the vice in one area, the authorities decreed that prostitution could be practiced in a designated district called "the Reservation," without risk of prosecution. The catch was that the girls had to stay on the Reservation. They were not permitted to leave it except to make occasional trips (in pairs) to buy necessities.

We are indebted to Ms. Johnson for evidence of yet another heart-of-gold whore, Madam Edna Ellmore, who owned and operated Twin Cottages at 438 North Second Street. The ambivalence of Waco's Baptist community toward prostitution is noted in Madam Ellmore's obituary which states: "She will be judged by a power that knows everything, and the deeds and the temptations will both be weighed. She never refused bread to the hungry and she visited the sick and ministered to them. Death is a leveler and purifier and in its awful presence let reproach be voiceless."

According to Aimee Johnson, Madam Ellmore "appears to be the classic whore with a heart of gold. Nevertheless, she was still a whore in the eyes of the community and her lifestyle was looked down on in the eyes of God."

Another madam who rated a star in her tarnished crown was Mollie Adams. Mollie had made a fortune in her brothels on three separate occasions and, in gratitude, made a special effort to relieve the boredom and drudgery of the profession for her girls. Because they were isolated in the Reservation area, she tried to create little social diversions for their entertainment, among them an annual picnic that was an eagerly anticipated event. She hired a hack to drive her girls to the banks of the Bosque River, just beyond the city limits—a propitious location because outside the city's boundaries they could not be harassed by the law for having strayed off the Reservation. There they waded in the river, played innocent picnic games, and enjoyed a day of ordinary family-style fun.

Mollie sat benignly by, contemplating the diamond rings that adorned most of her fingers and regretting her penchant for falling in love with men who were more interested in her money than her mind and heart. She paid the hack driver $10 for the round trip and gave him a $10 tip for treating her girls with kindness and courtesy.

And what does one eat at a parlor house picnic? Well, at that one the star attraction was Mollie Adams's special deviled eggs. There were sandwiches, of course, and Texas-fried chicken, baked ham, potato salad, pound cake, sweet potato pie, iced tea, lemonade, and beer.

Mollie Adams's Deviled Eggs

Mollie's picnic was for girls, but there's not a man alive who doesn't love deviled eggs. Just watch the fellows go for these when you serve them at a party.

12 eggs, hard cooked
½ cup light mayonnaise

THE BORDELLO Cookbook

¼ cup sweet pickle relish
1 teaspoon cider vinegar
1 teaspoon Dijon-style mustard
Salt and white pepper to taste
Dash hot sauce
Pimiento strips for garnish

Slice eggs in half lengthwise, and remove yolks. In a small bowl, mash yolks with mayonnaise. Add remaining ingredients, except pimientos, beating until mixture is light and smooth. Spoon yolk mixture into whites, garnish with a pimiento strip, or for more color, make an X, using 2 pimiento strips.

Yield: 24 deviled egg halves

Note: For fancy parties, pipe the filling into the egg white halves, using a pastry bag. Garnish with a sprinkling of black caviar.

Waco became a flash point for a self-styled "purity evangelist" named J. T. Upchurch when the city decided at the turn of the century to license prostitution. The city fathers reasoned that requiring prostitutes to obtain licenses would give Waco a measure of control over the vice as well as a new source of income. For $2.50, loosely the equivalent of $25 today, a girl could get a legal permit to conduct business for all of three months without risk of prosecution.

The girls cried "Foul!" and Upchurch charged through the street roaring "Hellfire and Damnation!" Of course nobody paid any attention to the girls, but Upchurch was such a rabid, nonstop crusader that ignoring him was not a possible thing. The holiness preacher was superintendent of the Home Mission and Rescue Commission of Texas, an organization of his own devising. He made a career of condemning and attempting to stamp out everything that he considered wicked and sinful, which was just about everything that appealed to Texans. His righteous wrath fell not only upon prostitution but pool, dominoes, horse racing, prize fighting, the Dallas Opera House, and make-believe plays of every kind, the ballroom (which he denounced as "The Devil's Reception Room"), chewing tobacco, whiskey, sweet wine, beer, dirty talk, fortune telling, and hypnotism.

Since it was easier to stop licensing prostitutes than to give up all of that, the Waco authorities caved in. The license law was revoked, Upchurch rejoiced, and Mollie Adams's girls had something special to celebrate at the next picnic.

Although time has marched on, Texans remain tolerant of the ancient profession. In Lubbock a few years back, Struggs Junior High School staged a history fair at which a shy fourteen-year-old seventh grader revealed a unique sense of history. For his project at the fair he built a bawdy house. The youngster constructed a scale model of a house similar to the notorious Chicken Ranch in La Grange. It was a gray, two-story structure with white trim, a red roof, and sugar cube chimney—and the house was authentically furnished, complete with

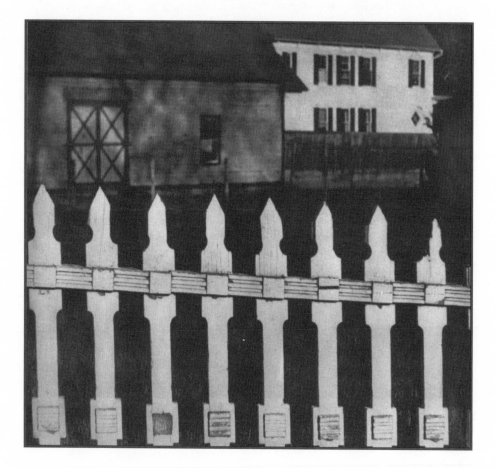

THE BORDELLO COOKBOOK

red lights, and "demonstrative pictures." The judges made him remove the pictures, but left the red lights intact and awarded his project first prize. Where did he get the idea? He said he "was not really sure" and his teachers expressed relief when he added "not at school." At any rate, he got his prize (a commemorative plaque), and his house was exhibited at the LBJ Library in Austin. On display also were the projects of twenty-nine other winners who had, predictably, built windmills and pueblos of sugar cubes and popsicle sticks, but they were hardly noticed. The crowds collected at guess where?—the Struggs Junior High red-lit bawdy house.

So much for Lone Star history. Texas forever!

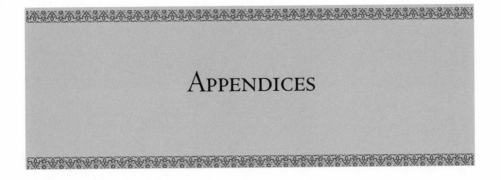

APPENDICES

Catalogue of Illustrations

Chapter Two

Chapter Three

Chapter Four

page 109: From an advertising plate of Domestic Animals, 1841, James Conner and Son, New York.

page 115: Nicholson, B.E. *Onions and Related Crops*, 1969.

page 118: French Pavilion, Louisiana Purchase Exposition, Saint Louis, Missouri, 1904, Library Picture Collection, Smithsonian Institution .

page 125: du Maurier, George. woodcut, *The Eton and Harrow Cricket Match at Lord's—Lookers-on*, 1871, London.

page 127: Photographer unknown. A Wedding, n.d.

Chapter Five

page 130: Photographer unknown. Cora Pearl, c. 1850, Mary Evans Picture Library.

page 133: Southworth, Albert Sands and Hawes, Josiah Johnson. Lola Montez, c. 1851, The Metropolitan Museum of Art, New York.

page 135: Pertschuk, Amy. *King Salmon*, (top), and *Silver Salmon*, (bottom), 1983.

page 137: Chase, William M. *The Blue Kimono*, c. 1898, The Parrish Art Museum, Southhampton, New York.

page 141: Bruce, Curt. 1745–1753 Pine Street, 1974, San Francisco.

page 143: Millais, Sir John Everett. woodcut illustration for *Once a Week*, 1862, London.

Chapter Six

page 148: Lartigue, Jacques Henri. Along the Bois Boulogne, c. 1910, Paris.

page 151: Morris, William. *Kelmscott Manor, from the Garth*, c. 1871.

page 152: Photographer unknown. 1920's style photograph of a sedan with passengers.

page 196: Lartigue, Jacques Henri. The Race Course at Auteuil, Paris, 1910, Museum of Modern Art, New York.

page 199: Klimt, Gustav. Portrait study, Profile of lady wearing hat and cape, 1897, Vienna.

page 205: Nicholson, B.E. *Some Plants of the Potato Family*, 1969.

page 208: Cassatt, Mary. *Young Women Picking Fruit*, 1891, Museum of Art, Carnegie Institute, Pittsburgh.

page 210: Strand, Paul. The White Fence, 1916, International Museum of Photography at George Eastman House, Rochester, New York.

INDEX